2012:
AWAKENING

2012:
AWAKENING

Choosing
Spiritual Enlightenment
Over Armageddon

Wisdom Teacher
Sri Ram Kaa
and Angelic Oracle Kira Raa

Ulysses Press

Published by:
ULYSSES PRESS
P.O. Box 3440
Berkeley, CA 94703
www.ulyssespress.com

ISBN10: 1-56975-678-3
ISBN13: 978-1-56975-678-2
Library of Congress Control Number: 2008904129

Printed in Canada by Transcontinental Printing

10 9 8 7 6 5 4 3

Acquisitions Editor: Nick Denton-Brown
Editor: Jo-Ann Langseth
Back cover and interior design and layout: whatdesign! @ whatweb.com
Front cover design: María Inés Montes

Distributed by Publishers Group West

CONTENTS

Chapter

ACKNOWLEDGMENTS

To bring forth a work of love and appreciation for our extraordinary world involves the energy and dedication of many. Our heart of Sacred Union reaches out with gratitude to those who remain unseen in our world of density, yet are creating miracles through all of us who choose to witness every moment of every day. This book is one of those miracles. Day by day we diligently bring forth the guidance of the Archangelic Realm and are assisted by many Angels in form at our ranch in New Mexico.

Our assistant, Delasaria, is a great gift of patience and love as she holds presence while we compile manuscripts, read and reread, until finally we can catch up with her very extensive and always well-ordered to-do list (even if it is on small sticky notes).

This particular book owes loving acknowledgment to Nick Denton-Brown at Ulysses Press. It was his diligence and commitment to bringing forth positive and unique perspectives on the vast subject of 2012 that left us with literally only one option, to offer this book to him for publication. Editor, Jo-Ann Langseth, offered invaluable assistance in clarifying the message and punctuation of this writing. Thank you both for believing in this project and for bringing it to form.

The work of the Archangelic Realm is supported by a group of amazing individuals known collectively as The Miracle Team. Each week they hold presence on behalf of the world, lovingly perform miracle manifestation energy without personal involvement, and open the portal for expansion of the work of the Archangelic Realm. We thank you all for your extraordinary love, trust, and momentum. We are at the time where each being on the planet is here to fully remember the gift that they are, and the presence of The Miracle Team in Action, is a miracle in and of itself.

And for you, our beloved readers of this book, thank you for trusting yourself enough to go on this journey at this very moment, right now. You will find within the journey many twists and turns, and yet may they all bring you home to the Truth that you are…a divine empowered gift of love, here on this planet, at this moment, right now…WE THANK YOU.

Many blessings of love,
Sri Ram Kaa and Kira Raa

FOREWORD

Our world is in transition. The energy of global change, like an unexpected storm, can sweep in and provoke fear and uncertainty. Just as every storm has a peaceful center, within every human heart is the doorway to Divine Peace. We each have the ability to choose an ascended perspective toward the events of the outer world, and thus we each can align with a greater Wisdom, should we wish to claim dominion over our own consciousness.

As we travel the world speaking with thousands of people, the questions that arise have a common denominator. People need reassurance that they can trust their inner knowing, and reassurance that there is an Intelligence underpinning what is happening in our world. Audiences worldwide want to know that they are not crazy, and that the Spiritual Realms are indeed talking to us more directly now than ever before. We are at a great time in human history—the major turn in the cycle of the ages. Mass Consciousness is indeed shifting and expanding, and unless we find new perspectives, the coming years will be a "white-knuckles ride!"

Our first book on this topic, *2012: You Have a Choice!*, offered foundational teachings and insights around the coming shift in consciousness. We have woven much of the material presented there into this current work and expanded upon those themes. This work includes fresh insights that we have gained through our public appearances and workshops so that you, the reader, have timely information.

There are many authors who write brilliant interpretations of the Mayan records, and illuminate other prophecies. These works can provide an interesting context for our era. However, it is clear to us that there is no roadmap for this time in history. We are literally writing the map as we go. Therefore, it is time to bring our full co-creative power and intuitive wisdom to bear upon the choices we are making as individuals and as a society. The power of conscious choice and focused intention has never been greater. We are the Ones who will collectively decide our pathway through the coming times. Let us awaken to our highest potential now!

With great love from TOSA ranch, New Mexico, 2008,
Sri Ram Kaa & Kira Raa

A MESSAGE FROM THE HOPI

We have been telling the people that this is the Eleventh Hour. Now you must go back and tell the people that this is THE HOUR. And there are things to be considered...

Where are you living? What are you doing? What are your relationships? Are you in the right relation? Where is your water? Know your garden. It is time to speak your truth. Create your community. Be good to each other. And do not look outside yourself for the leader.

This could be a good time!

There is a river flowing now very fast. It is so great and swift that there are those who will be afraid. They will try to hold on to the shore. They will feel they are being torn apart and they will suffer greatly. Know the river has its destination. The Elders say we must let go of the shore, and push off and into the river, keep our eyes open, and our head above the water. See who is in there with you, and celebrate.

At this time in history, we are to take nothing personally, least of all ourselves. For the moment that we do, our spiritual growth and journey come to a halt. The time of the lone wolf is over. Gather yourselves! Banish the word struggle from your attitude and your vocabulary. All that you do now must be done in a sacred manner and in celebration.

"We are the ones we've been waiting for..."

The Elders, Hopi Nation, Oraibi, Arizona

INTRODUCTION
by William J. Birnes, Ph.D.

Sri Ram Kaa and Kira Raa appeared on the scene of the Consciousness Movement in 2003. Since that time they have produced four books and countless workshops, all designed to empower people to trust their inner knowing. Their message of empowered Love and Joy has touched the hearts of many thousands of people worldwide. If you have not read their previous books, then you have a treat in store. All of their writings offer a very special journey, a treasure you will appreciate the more you read—and I urge you to read more!

Sri and Kira show readers how to discover their own pathways through time and across boundaries of space, as well as millennia. The exercises that they lay out for readers in this book illustrate that what seems like an impossibility is, in fact, a straightforward process of finding truth that is already there. Their own trust in the divine opens a portal of Archangelic connection that illuminates their teachings and inspires us to remember that we are not alone in the universe.

As you read *2012*, you will learn to trust your instincts more and more. Sri and Kira inspire us to align of lives with our own authentic knowing and discover that we are indeed Divine Co-creators. Transcending religion, Sri and Kira's message reminds us that our Souls' wisdom is accessible and, by trusting that wisdom we will all find our way through the challenges ahead.

You will learn that love is the strongest force in the universe, and that love, when embraced for the joy that it is, nurtures all. Know that if you are reading this, you will be nurtured, for you are already home.

William J. Birnes is the *New York Times* bestselling co-author of *The Day After Roswell* with Lt. Col. Philip J. Corso. Birnes has contributed to over 25 books in the field of human behavior, produces the History Channel's UFO Hunters TV show and publishes *UFO Magazine*. His newest book, *Workers In The Light*, was co-authored with George Noory of Coast to Coast AM Radio. Birnes lives in Los Angeles and New York with his wife, novelist and editor Nancy Hayfield.

Chapter One

LIVING IN A WORLD AT CHOICE-POINT

Nostradamus…Biblical revelations…Hopi prophecy…the end of the Kali Yuga…the Mayan calendar; the range of prophetic information about this very moment in our collective history is extensive. Most likely you are familiar with at least one if not all of the above-mentioned, and many other widely circulated and popularly accepted premonitory works about 2012. As you review this short yet well-known list of 2012 prophecies, what emotions, thoughts, or reactions immediately come to the forefront of your consciousness? Are they positive or negative? A little of both? Are your emotions, thoughts, and reactions clear, or are they confused? Do they seek resolution, or do you have a strong sense of what is true based upon your interactions with them?

Taking a moment to find the answers to these important questions is the beginning of a journey that you decided to participate in a long time ago, a decision that is manifesting now. Perhaps you are one of the many who, since birth, have always had a feeling or knowing about our world and its immediate future. There is great strength in the recognition that everything in our world is rapidly escalating to a heightened sense of presence that pervades all thoughts, discussions, prayers, and sensations. That is, regardless of your religious beliefs, political affiliations, or consciousness, the one thing we can all agree on is that our world cannot go on the way things are.

Let's look at some of the facts.

- Our world is finally accepting that global warming is real.
- We have overpopulated our planet and must pay attention to how she can continue to sustain us all.
- The rise in fundamentalism in all aspects and forms is stirring conflict, and impelling everyone to pay attention.
- Democratic elections in the U.S. feel staged and inauthentic, while voter participation is at an all-time low.
- More people than ever before have a conscious understanding of the Law of Attraction and know that spiritual energy can affect the physical world.

The above statements are just that—statements. They are presented without judgment simply to offer a reality check as to what is around us. When we can refer to these facts without any reaction, we are able to receive the gift of these facts, and the many other challenges that we are faced with on a daily basis.

For just this moment, consider the extraordinary opportunity they offer. These often grimly presented facts about our world are forcing everyone, like it or not, to finally and completely wake up from complacency in all of its forms! This is cause for true celebration.

Regardless of your reaction or nonreaction to the situations in our world, the bigger picture is emerging through you and as you. Your consciousness does affect our shared world. The ultimate paradigm-buster is at hand, and you chose to be here, on this planet, right now, as part of the shift.

In a world that has brought us Star Trek....Star Wars...Star Gate...there is...also...You. What if, just for a moment, you *knew that the science fiction was not all a myth?* What if you allowed yourself the possibility that you are on a Divine Galactic Mission? What if this journey began eons ago, expanded through millennia, and is now ready to go into hyperdrive?

ARE YOU READY TO FULLY AWAKEN FROM THE DREAM?

Ready or not, you are waking up! The journey of many millennia is about to expand into infinite expressions, and you are on this ride, like it or not. Regardless of what you may believe at this moment, you wanted to be on this ride. It is the reason you are here. It is why you are on this particular planet at this exact moment in history.

IN FACT, IT IS WHY YOU ARE READING THIS BOOK, RIGHT NOW!

Whether you purchased this book yourself, borrowed it from a friend, or find yourself reviewing it out of perceived obligation, the fact is, you are here, right now.

Choice is a gift, and we are at the time of great decisions. You are continually called to choose simply by virtue of being alive. Every day you must make countless choices. You decide when to get out of bed, what to eat, what to wear. This powerful energetic tool that we call **choice** is the natural evolution of free will, and is a great asset for this planet. It is time to become much more conscious of the choices we are making.

We have all been bombarded with choice-making scenarios since the moment of birth, and before. Our ability to make wise choices affects everything we experience. As computer technology increases and communications are increasingly refined, we become more adept at making quick decisions. Consider that not too many years ago, the fax machine was a revolution and the Internet did not exist. Computer research and real-time news reports influence our decisions. For many people, computers now offer a substitute for independent thinking.

All these life choices pale in comparison to the choice that is upon you in this moment. The grandest choice, the greatest choice, and the single most important choice is the one that you have spent lifetimes preparing for, and are now ready to make. It is the reason you picked up this book, and the primary reason we were asked to write it.

In the same world that brought us *The Matrix*,[1] with red and blue pill options, and in a world that numbs us with thousands of marketing messages each day, you have the wondrous ability to claim your soul's choice. This choice determines how you will complete your time on this planet, in this world, in this existence. It is one of the most important choices before you. Are you listening?

Your soul is stepping forward. The still, small voice within your heart is ready to be heard. Are you willing to listen? Are you ready to discern your inner truth and make a conscious decision?

Every moment is the result of your choices, the most exciting part being the awareness that all choices are perfect. Imagine the freedom you can experience knowing that every choice you make is absolutely correct! There is no need to second-guess yourself, especially if you listen to your heart prior to choosing.

Consider this perspective: You are doing the best you can at every moment, given the state of your consciousness at the time. Therefore, you are always at your best! Only our self-judgment, combined with a false sense of time, causes us to second-guess our choices.

"What if you chose to believe that everything in your world was perfect, as is, right now? What if you implicitly trusted your inner guidance system to produce the words and actions needed in any situation you found yourself?

What if every moment was guided by the One who truly loves you?"

Eastern religions and cultures have long accepted that we live many lifetimes, reincarnating into a body over and over again. You may also already accept this notion, and you may not. However, let's play along for a moment and consider: What if this is really true? Then, it is also quite possible that we have lived in many worlds throughout the universe, incarnating into form, having experiences, and awakening to our spiritual self, time and time again.

Whether or not the above is a paradigm-buster for you, the concept of expanding your recognition of self and life beyond this world involves a sense of deepening trust in your own sense of knowing and interacting with the world. Throughout this book we will take you on a journey that will most likely cause you to stop, consider, and go beyond the words into that sacred place known as your heart.

To fully explore your heart is a journey that can be invited only by your recognition that the mind can bring you only so far. Perhaps our world is ready to journey beyond its conceptualizations and enter into a space that is beyond our ability to fathom from our earthbound perspective. Therefore, we must enter through another door, one that we have used successfully before, and are ready to fully embrace again.

However, the gatekeeper of this door is a powerful opponent, one that has, by design, done its best to keep us from walking through! Alive within us, this opponent has often demonstrated that it is a good keeper of our safety and yet has led to great separation on many levels of our experience. Who is this opponent? You are…when you allow yourself to doubt your ability to clearly and accurately discern all answers, all knowledge, and all wisdom. This separation began when you stopped trusting yourself.

Trust me! These two words immediately provoke a reaction in both sender and receiver. More than ever, this is a phrase that most often evokes fear and suspicion in the one being asked to trust, and frustration in the one who is seeking your trust in some important sharing. It seems that we have collectively accepted the norm of setting aside our essential trust in humanity and instead lead with suspicion and doubt. After all, is that not the predominant energy being offered through our mainstream media?

What is it about our world that has encouraged our interactions with others to lean toward the energy of "guilty until proven innocent?" Words are just that—words. It is the energy that fuels our interactions that has brought us to this choice-point for humanity. Further, we now seem to require and solely rely upon what we deem to be "expert" advice before making any and all decisions.

Why have we given away our true power to so-called experts who we believe must know more than ourselves? When did we so willingly lose connection with our inner knowing and our inner conscience? This separation from our intuitive knowing also perpetuates and fuels the debate about and the demand for "evidence" of otherworldly life, spiritual connections and visions, and anything that our scientific community deems unverifiable via the accepted "scientific method!" (Of course, as touted by the "experts.")

You chose to be reading this book now. Congratulate yourself. Whether you are somewhat familiar with the content or are just now opening yourself to a new possibility, the gift in this moment is that, conscious or not, you are aware that there is a much greater force at work here. And you are allowing that force to work through you...a basis of divine trust! This force is greater than our day-to-day lives and interactions, greater than our belief or unbelief in UFOs, Angels, prophecies, visions, crop circles, etc. This force calls forth the greatest battle of all...the battle to regain dominion of our own consciousness! Yes, dominion.

Consider the meaning of dominion. Our dictionaries define dominion as having ruling control, or a sphere of influence. Often dominion is sought or struggled for with the energy of righteousness... That is, we seek to exert dominion over another, or dominion over a situation in an effort to prove our authority or influence.

In spite of the extraordinary range of mounting evidence (scientific, empirical, and other) that has been presented regarding otherworldly existence, and the increasing validity of spiritual contact at all levels, for the most part, people seem to enjoy letting others have dominion over their lives, thus inviting and allowing "authorities" to define what is real for them. This disavowal of our own personal authority and inner knowing always comes into play with any topic that significantly challenges established paradigms. Why is that? Perhaps there really is some **thing**, whether internal or external, that wants to limit human perception. While this can be challenging to look at, because it means we must look at ourselves, let's take a moment and go on a journey together.

Let's begin with just a deep loving breath that is felt throughout the body. Yes, right now. As you allow this breath to complete, reconnect with the last experience you had that made you feel absolutely wonderful. A recent moment of discovery or recognition that brought you great joy. As you reconnect with this interaction, you recognize that this experience carried with it a strong sense of undeniable knowing within your heart. There was a certainty that you felt around this situation that was instinctual. It was real...on all levels. Sincerely take a moment and bring this experience forward for yourself right now. Maybe it was a personal interaction with spirit or a friend, a beautiful nature experience, or an "ah-hah" moment of realization. Maybe it was the 2008 UFO sightings in Texas, or an encounter you witnessed in the night sky. The event does not matter—**what you felt, does.**

Now...**and pay attention here**...in the spirit of your joy, did you find yourself sharing your enthusiasm with another, or did you feel obliged to "research" your instinctual knowing? While you may sincerely believe you were just sharing your wonderful experience, can you begin to recognize that deep within you was the need to seek outside validation? This is an important discernment because it gives rise to the greater perspective.

Reflect on your sharing... Did those whom you shared with respond with skepticism, or were they able to support and celebrate your understanding? Did you receive sarcastic or dismissive feedback from another person? Did you uncover a blog site of negative comments around similar experiences, and find yourself compelled to read them all?

These are THE important questions. Why? Because it is how you choose to respond to them that will open your door to greater self-trust, and uncover doubts that you may not know are harbored within you. Remember, it is the energy of your experience calling you forward. The words have no meaning, especially those we use to delude ourselves. Consider this for a moment: What if those who seek to interfere with your truth know that the dominion of your brain is actually theirs to influence because you have willingly given your power away? What if you became aware of this oppositional energy and were able to take back dominion of your brain, your consciousness, and the authenticity that is your life?

WHAT IF THAT TIME IS RIGHT NOW?

The 2008 UFO "megasighting" in Texas is a great and powerful call to self-trust. Within this one defining moment, all of these elements came together for the world to witness and respond to. Let's begin with those tenuous witnesses who were terrified to share what they saw, and only came forward when others did. This is a vivid display of their recognition (even if subconsciously) that they are ready to reclaim their dominion. Those who came forward first released their self-doubt and fear of public ridicule; they KNOW they did not see two airliners reflecting lights, and they KNOW that they are treading in a new area of self-acceptance. They also know that although it feels terrible to be dismissed and ridiculed, their greater knowing would have to come forward. This is true freedom.

True freedom will not ever be granted to you by a government, a country, a friend, or a relative. True freedom is yours when you begin to trust yourself and what you experience. When you can accept that self-doubt is the best weapon in the battle for your brain among those who would seek to control it, you begin to embrace true freedom and regain dominion of your own life!

Guilty until proven innocent; is that really how we want to live? Is that really the world we wish to sustain: an environment that perpetuates disempowerment from our own self-truth through slick media, moral spin, and disinformation campaigns? Why not allow this monumental recognition to be the stimulus to say *Enough! I choose true freedom!*

Perhaps the greatest gift available to us all in this moment is that we can use the disinformation and repressive energy to stimulate new and greater clarity. Train yourself to let your inner thoughts declare: I am ready to actually believe myself; I deserve to trust what I know and to celebrate others who are doing the same! I AM FREE.

There is no doubt that our world is approaching a new gateway to freedom and enlightened action. It is truly our "If not now... When?" moment of humanity. We are ALL at a choice-point, for if we choose to deepen our self-trust we will then collaborate together in new and authentic ways. If we hesitate or decide not to make this choice, then the future, based upon the trends already in place, is quite predictable.

Multidimensional, interdimensional, and spiritual contact has happened and is happening. Those who seek to contact us through their subtle and noninvasive means offer a benevolent energy that stimulates us to claim our knowing. They are each giving us a gift, the undeniable opportunity to claim back the truth of what we know and who we are. Are you ready to claim the true freedom that is yours to live?

As we become receptive to deeper self-trust, new information, and our own inner wisdom, the quality of our choices is enhanced. We become conscious, loving Co-Creators. As such, we can assimilate new information, discard the pieces that don't feel congruent, and move forward in life with confidence. This is the path of living a soul-based life. It is an orientation that trusts our inner wisdom, and finely hones our discernment to navigate the outer world without being controlled by it. From this place, we anchor our hearts as the truth detector of all prophecy.

Walk through this book and continue this journey. You will be delighted, and you will be intrigued. Perhaps you may be challenged. Most importantly, you will gain new information that will assist you to clearly make a critical choice.

Remember that there are no wrong choices. As Archangel Zadkiel so lovingly reminds us, *If at any time you question the choice you are making, it is confirmation that you are on the right path!* When you question, you are simply loving yourself enough to ask your guidance system for reassurance. Only you can give yourself this gift of choice.

Chapter Two

ARE WE REALLY THAT POWERFUL?

By now you are asking, "What is this 2012 choice, and how do I make it?" This is a question simply asked, and one this book seeks to assist you in answering. The challenge before us is that the choice facing you and all of humanity is clouded in myth, mystery, dogma, and distortion. These veils make it very difficult to discern the truth.

We will do our best to offer clear information that will assist you. As with all meaningful decisions, it is best if we avoid oversimplifying the situation, at least until you have a sense of what brought you to this choice-point. Ultimately, your inner wisdom and your own heart will make the decision in an instant. Living with our decisions takes commitment and focus! By the time you complete this journey with us, your mind will have more clarity, your heart will discern the truth, and your soul will offer you the answer.

Some of you may be wondering if you can trust what is written here. We only ask that you trust yourself. Throughout this book we ask you to listen to your inner knowing and trust your own heart. We will offer information that might shock you. We will lovingly challenge some of your beliefs, and confirm some of your suspicions! Trust yourself enough to know that you can handle anything this book has to say, and give yourself permission to reignite your imagination, if need be...

Consider that just 520 years ago people **knew** the world was flat. For centuries it was considered to be fact that the sun rotated around the Earth. Just 120 years ago the idea that machines would fly people across continents was pure fantasy. By reflecting on the expansion of human awareness and the quantum growth of technology in recent years, we see that new understandings are obliterating old beliefs. New "facts" replace old "facts." Little wonder there is an upsurge in fundamentalism of all types, for change in the outer world creates discomfort when it fails to conform to our accepted belief patterns. The world is changing and belief systems are being shaken.

By gifting yourself with reading this book, you will share the journey of Sri Ram Kaa and Kira Raa. These two people came together during midlife, embraced the mission placed in front of them, and surrendered what many call "normal" lives. This is also the journey of an Archangel named Zadkiel,[2] who lovingly offers profound assistance at this time in the Earth's history.

The story of how Archangel Zadkiel, a Being of great love, wisdom, and compassion, came to speak through Kira Raa is shared in our first book, *Sacred Union: The Journey Home.* We now understand that by opening ourselves fully to the Archangelic Presence, we have reconnected with Angelic In-soulment.[3] This is not channeling, a common New Age practice. Rather, it is a direct interdimensional communion and the result of complete surrender and trust in God. In-soulment is a sacred gift that offers reconnection to benevolent energy and galactic wisdom that modern society has long forgotten and yet, not too long ago on our planet, was lovingly revered and recognized for centuries.

Time magazine has reported that over 75% of Americans believe in Angels.[4] However, we have witnessed that many of these same people scoff at the idea that an Archangel would consistently and with great clarity communicate through and with a modern human, much less an American woman.

The miracle is not that Angels are very real; the miracle is that we are even able to notice them and to trust them. Most modernized people have become so separated from their hearts, and so entrenched in the technological numbing of the modern world, that their abilities to discern the subtle Realms are dormant. They simply cannot see or sense the energy of a Being who is not in a body. However, nuns, monks, and disciplined students of meditation have often been exposed to Angelic Beings and other energies that don't have bodies as we define them. Every major spiritual tradition speaks of these Angelic Beings in one way or another. There is an important discernment to be made here, which is that many of these Angelic visions were actually experienced through the receiver having opened clairvoyant sight through many different means. This is very different from the perception that the Angel appeared in form, as commonly expressed in literal translations. The context of understanding these visitations is a powerful gift, for it frees the mind to ALL experience. This is not to say that full-body manifestations have not occurred; we simply wish to express that each being is capable of a greater experience of contact when there is willingness to trust oneself enough to relax into spaciousness and expanded perceptions.

Metaphysical information gathered through our communion with Ascended Beings offers an opportunity to open to higher wisdom. It broadens the context for our earthly struggles and opens us to a greater appreciation of this life experience and the ALL that is. However, the information received must pass the test of your own heart. All too often people rely on external authorities—this may be wise when it comes to repairing a machine, but it is not wise when it comes to making life decisions.

Your life is a precious gift, an opportunity for your soul to interact with others and to expand in love. The greatest gift you can give yourself and the universe is to be guided by your authentic inner knowing, and to not robotically follow someone else's prescription. Through your authenticity you may find yourself aligned with many other people. The key is that you are aligned through conscious knowing, not conformity or obligation.

This text was created for those who are seeking greater self-illumination and freedom. It was designed for those who are exploring their own knowing. We learn best through contrast and sincere investigation.

Modern media has made us cynical. News is presented or spun to promote a certain point of view. Our attention is manipulated to witness some events at the expense of other events. We are taught to suspect others until they have earned our trust. In a world of words, how does one choose what and whom to trust? There is only one healthy solution: Cultivate trust in your own heart, and from that inner knowing you can discern what is healthy for you to trust in the outer world.

Regardless of whether you gain information from a scientific source or inner inspiration, you must choose what you will accept. The mind by itself is limited, for it accepts information that has intellectual "proof" only. However, the heart has access to the soul, the essential you, which some people refer to as the Higher Self. If you open the doorway to your heart's knowing, you can test any information you receive against the wisdom of your immortal soul. This is the one and only authentic lie detector, and it will never fail you.

Many are waking up to the fact that we are not just physical beings; we are more than our bodies. Many more are starting to acknowledge that our consciousness is not limited to our personal space, and that we can project our awareness to many other "places." The marked increase and interest in remote viewing, psychic phenomena, the new field of medical intuition—all point to the expansion of human consciousness beyond conventional boundaries. We are at a time in which so many are having the same experience that the possibility of collective delusion must be discarded, and the recognition that we are awakening beyond the paradigm of old traditions is now.

When Archangel Zadkiel first offered assistance to us, we were delighted, yet dubious. Could we trust this Being? Could we trust the information and the process of receiving the information? Obviously, we did; however, getting to that place of deep trust challenged most everything we once held as true. Zadkiel has patiently accompanied us as we incorporated his information and guidance. Despite procrastination and ego testing, we have found that God does speak through

Angels, and we can know what is true by letting the words fall on our own hearts.

We invite you to do your best to separate the message from the messenger. That is, if you for any reason find it challenging to accept that our source of loving and divine inspiration is an Archangel, then please just suspend that concern. Read the messages as they are presented, and allow yourself to discover if there is something there for you. Whether the inspired material comes from an Archangel or an inner passion is not as important to discern as the gift of the information being shared.

When we share information received directly from the Archangelic Realm, we have not edited the Angelic communications for grammar or content. Changing their words would shift the message to fit an intellectual model. We respect you enough to trust that you will find the meaning that is yours to receive without our editing or interpretations.

This painting of Archangel Zadkiel was found in Peru by Sri and Kira.

WHAT IS ARCHANGELIC IN-SOULMENT?

Archangelic In-soulment is not channeling. Channeling is when a stream of information, or an energy, enters a person's mind, offering a felt sense, visual stream, sounds, and/or world. This inner data must be faithfully received by the person channeling before the mind jumps in and paints an interpretation of the inspiration. Channeling is therefore subject to possible distortion by the mind of the receiver. This does not make it false. It is more like trying to convert poetry to prose, whereby the essential message is clouded by an unintentional distortion in the translation.

It is challenging to restrain the mind; it does take practice. It is natural to want to be able to communicate the vision, to share the details with others. In a spoken channel, there is a blended energy wherein the automatic responses of the mind join with the pure stream of channeled energy. Channeling offers a message of interdimensional information blended with Earth-based distortions. As the ego feels the inspiration, it may naturally become proud and feel special, which is how further distortions may creep in. The mind is easily influenced by the ego, but the heart is not as easily misled. This is why we recommend that you listen with your heart and not be seduced by the words alone. Your heart is your most trusted guide.

When the Archangelic stream communicates through Kira Raa, the only word that initially came to mind to describe the process was "channeling." Yet, something very different is happening here. Her body literally goes limp, for several moments her breathing stops, as in the dying process, and there is complete absence of her personality and voice. Her ability to move the body is gone. For all practical purposes, Kira dies, and then the Archangelic energy animates her body. The tangible energy of the communication that follows is far beyond words. That is, the radiance of love is so tangible that the words shared are actually a bonus and not the sole reward of the communication! Kira always returns without any recollection of the message delivered. The experience is far more than an inspired dance of words; it is the felt presence of Divine Communion.

This is a process that we actually embrace together. Each time Kira Raa leaves her body to allow for the Angelic Presence to enter, her soul literally comes home to Sri Ram Kaa's soul. Later in this book you will learn about the Union soul, which we are. Together, we complete the process of Archangelic Communion, and together we have learned how to live with it.

Two years into our communications with the Archangelic Realm, Helena Blavatsky[5] revealed herself to us during a session, and directed us to an understanding of **In-souling**. At length, she shared that during her time on the planet, the wisdom she brought through was largely misunderstood and her spiritual gifts often discounted. And no matter how many miracles appeared, there was a constant call for more. Yet, she appeared as a means of comfort to Kira Raa and me, for she understood through her life that sharing the Archangelic information would expose us to many judgments and misunderstandings. She reminded us that the information we were receiving was for the benefit of many, to not hold back, and that the timing of the sharing was important.

Uniquely different from channeling, In-souling is direct communion of one soul with another, an ancient process of Angelic communication that completely removes egoic barriers. Kira Raa has learned how to leave her body to fully allow the Angelic Presence to enter. She was trained for this through several near-death experiences. Therefore, her ability to In-soul provides the fullest expression of the Divine Presence without any density-ego to distort information.

We have witnessed many Angelic miracles during these In-soulment sessions. Many have had instantaneous physical and emotional healings. Front-row attendees have walked away with what appeared to be sunburn on their faces. Kira's eyes are always very wide open during the In-soulment, and the energy transmitted through them has brought many to spontaneous recognition of their own divinity.

Reflect for a moment on how the filament of a light bulb behaves: It glows from the input of energy. The filament serves as a point of resistance to offer the light. If the resistance is too great, there is only heat and burning and not much expression of light. Just like Thomas Edison trying hundreds of possible filaments, Kira and I have had to make hundreds of changes in our food intake and our living environment in order to offer a pure expression of Archangelic In-souling. These sessions can be very taxing to the physical body; thus we have eliminated all contaminants of a typical modern environment, such as processed foods and polluted water, and we have purified our vessels through a commitment to organic vegetarian nourishment and regular fasting.

Without great purity in her nourishment and living environment, Kira's body would, in a short time, simply wear out. Just like the filament with too much resistance, the contaminants would block the flow of Angelic expression, thus either inhibiting the transmission or burning up in the face of the Divine energy, thereby wearing down the physical vessel. Prompted by the loving suggestions of our Archangelic Guides, we have fasted, purified, and adjusted our nourishment to make living our mission here on Earth as comfortable as is possible.

After several years of living with this energy on a daily basis, we have let go of the need to define it, and have simply accepted the Presence as the gift that it is. We have dedicated our lives to this communion and to traveling the world to share this gift. Know that we are grateful to be sharing it with you.

Enjoy the miracle of direct Archangelic Communication. Read those passages twice or more to let the intent behind the message wash over you. Make your own decisions about the meaning of the information. Let this book help you ground more fully in your own heart by showing you what you will trust and what you do not. Whether you want to learn more or throw the book in the trash is up to you. We celebrate your ability to know what is right for you at this time.

If you are having difficulty accepting what we write yet still find yourself curious or intrigued, we suggest that you just "pretend." Allow yourself to read this book as if it were an adventure or fairy tale. Let your imagination play with the information and set aside any need to decide if it is true. We are not asking you to believe us. We are only requesting that you listen to the perspective we share and then notice what arises in you.

The year 2012, our collective world, our living or energetic vibration, our soul evolution, and our very existence are tied to the choice that you make now. We are all influenced by one another, and we owe it to ourselves to honor the decisions of others. Know that within every choice is great power. The choices that create the greatest impact are those that require us to stretch beyond our familiar boundaries.

Who could ever forget the momentous decision made by Indiana Jones as he chose to make a dramatic leap of faith in the movie *Indiana Jones and the Last Crusade*?[6] Frantically reading through his father's notebook while seeing his destination before him, he stands before a vast crevasse of certain death. Summoning great trust, he tucks the book of notes into his shirt, sticks out his foot, and leaps! We all held our breath, waiting to see what would happen next.

It was only then that the bridge appeared, revealing itself because he'd made a clear choice and held the conviction of that choice without reservation. It was only as he placed one foot out in front of the other that the path appeared. This scene captured the truth of spiritual surrender.

Throughout this book you will find questions (many from people just like you), Archangelic discourses, dialogues, and suggested practices. With Zadkiel's help, we are opening the doors to a Galactic re-connection. More than a "citizen" of this world, embrace the possibility of becoming a *responsible, loving Galactic* citizen. Open your heart to expansiveness and opportunity that is not limited by lifespan, health, gravity, or finances. Use this material to help you decide for yourself what you will trust. If anything you read becomes too challenging, then invite in the process of imagination. Gift yourself with permission to simply pretend, as if you were reading a fable.

Most importantly, enjoy the process! You may find that new insight is shed on these perennial questions: "Why am I here, alive on Earth? What is my service?" It is our hope that you will listen to your Awakened Heart, connect with your inner wisdom, and make your choice to walk confidently through the times ahead, feeling the Joy of your Divine Connection.

There are no secrets.

~ARCHANGEL ZADKIEL

It is a magnificent time to be alive. It is a magnificent and glorious time to know the gifts that are abundant here on this planet Earth. It is a glorious time to celebrate all that is manifesting, manifested, and in the process of culminating now. Be joyous. Be in joy, for it is the time of the glorious manifestation of all of the products, services, trainings, and needed things to continue. Know this. The people, the places, the things, as they say, are all here, are already aligned; even those you have not met yet are already aligned. They are ready and waiting, and those you have met are ready and waiting, ready to shift.

It is a glorious time to be alive and understand the many gifts that we are given on a continuous basis from the Oneness, from the Light, the Love. The Universal secrets, as they say, are ever available to all. They are only a secret because one chooses not to know. So it is, when anything becomes available to knowing, it is no longer a secret. Many talk about holding the secret, they know a secret, they offer the secret, they will tell you the secret, it is a special secret, oh my goodness. This word secret used much.

The secret is not so much in the knowing as it is in the Being.

When one is being, then one understands. If one is allowing, if one is in surrender, then one can be. When one has the secret, it means that they are still withholding from themselves, from others, from the world.

There is no basis for this withholding unless one desires power of control. The Elohim[7] does not desire power or control; this is why there can be no secret. The only gift that the Elohim offer is the expanding Love of Light. That is the big secret!

You are an expansion of Love. You are expanding, and as Light, everything becomes available for you to see. Understand the metaphor of what we say, for we can only offer metaphors because in our Realm it is challenging to discuss, disseminate, or offer this information in a way that would satisfy the density brain. Yet we must, for you are still in this vessel.

SRI RAM KAA: So throughout the last several thousand years, there have been secret teachings, mystery schools, and secret societies. It is my understanding that they were secret because it was not safe for them to be out in the open.

*Yes, this is true. This is very true; however, let us explore this a little more. There are those who hold in secret their training even to the sincere seeker of the secret because of a need to have a structured or uniform process whereby they feel it must be approved to divulge their secret. While this has had its place and certainly was formed with good intent, it is important to understand that the true seeker can find any secret at any time by going into their heart and connecting. One can access **All** by genuinely and sincerely saying, "Dearest God, my heart is open, I am here, I am ready, I am open, guide me."*[8]

We offer you this information because the time of the secret has passed. The secret is out, as they say. Everything is out in this world; very little is no longer out. Oh yes, there are still some things to be, as you would say, discovered, or recovered is more accurate. Soon they will find things that will be indisputable, although they will want to dispute, of course. It will become very evident there was life on Mars.[9] *They are already getting it, yet it will not be released to the public for quite a while. However, it already exists.*

SRI RAM KAA: The data?

Yes, the pictures.

SRI RAM KAA: The pyramids?

Yes, and beyond. There is more than one reason they now wish to send someone there.

SRI RAM KAA: That's traveling the hard way.

Yes, it is. Of course it is, because it comes from a method of density and scientific experimentation that is unlike light; however, it serves its purpose. Know this, it is the time of the great awakening, it is the time of the great Self-Ascension, it is the time of the knowing of all secrets, of the revealing of ancient mystery wisdom, whichever you wish to call it, that will offer much release of judgment to many. For you see, the only time capsule that needs to be unburied here is the one that inside contains the unconditional love for the Self, for the world. It has been long buried!

When you and Kira came back together you were part of the activation of this time capsule opening. It is that deep, deep love between each of you that continues to unlock this capsule and bring it out. Those around you will feel it, know it, and express it, especially those of open pure heart. This is your work. You will attract those of open pure heart, and you will open many hearts. You will reveal, for lack of a better word, what they consider to be secrets. This will be very exciting. Everyone wants to know the secret. Yet it is important for them to understand that the only secret is the one they keep from themselves.

This is the only key that is needed: to unlock a heart. You are in a society, you are in a modern age that is paced at a speed that is not healthy, that does not support unconditional love. In this world, unconditional love is subject to time. Time is a false God. Everything subjected to time becomes conditional. There is no time to love you unconditionally; I must be at an appointment. There is no time for me to be myself because I must be someone else for this period of time or to do this or make this money, whatever.

That is the great secret, to unlock the heart, and allow the floodgate of unconditional love for the Self to open. Forgive, and reemerge as the soul-based, heart-centered, Self-Ascended energy, ready to be of service to all. Be in the continuous flow of the God of Love.

Sri & Kira at an Archangelic In-soulment

NOTHING HAPPENS WITHOUT YOUR PARTICIPATION.

Fear spawns actions that carry a wounding energy. Judgment carries a wounding energy. We all can agree that being judged or experiencing fear collapses us and makes us feel smaller in some way. Thus, every world event that collapses our energy, that spawns fear and doubt, can cause us to disconnect from true Peace and the authenticity of Love.

The more we agree to accept the perspective that results in fear, the more we empower a destructive pattern already established in our shared world. When we read the news, we empower those stories to be true. We literally give them power.

The Law of Attraction is universal and indifferent: We attract more of that which we focus upon. If we focus upon joy and Spirit expressing in form, then we'll attract more Joy and Conscious Recognition into our world. If we focus on the struggle and heartache that is also present, then we'll attract more of that.

It is important to remember that the Law of Attraction operates according to your energy and focus. Seeing pain in our world does not alone make more pain. Fearing the pain does. The energy of fear seeks an object to latch on to and "be afraid of," thus empowering that object to keep existing.

Love does the same. If you love a certain color, you'll start seeing it more often. If you love certain types of situations, then you'll start attracting those situations into your life—provided that you also take action each time you recognize that they are headed your way. You see, the Law of Attraction requires continuing participation. If you doubt that it works, you'll get more doubt in your life. If you trust your co-creative power for a while, the universe will start organizing itself around your intention. But if you subsequently change your mind, the universe unravels what it started and you then receive an unclear response. To create intentional change requires consistent commitment.

Given that the outer world will conform to your focused intentions, then it is a simple matter to obtain a life experience that you'll enjoy. The only caveat is to watch that your attention is not interfered with. Co-creation is based upon a state of peaceful knowingness, a state of being that can see and trust that what is desired is truly available and yours.

Try holding that state of peaceful knowing in a world full of blasting ad campaigns, wars, bank failures, crime, unrest…etc. Get the picture? The outer world is already programmed to perpetuate chaos.

You can change this. To do so, you must first change your inner world. If you can hold a peaceful center, a state of beingness that trusts in the Divine, then your energy field will radiate a calming force into the sea of polarity. If enough people truly anchor this peaceful trust in the Divine, then we will all see a shift in the trends started in our world and begin a new trend toward coherence and harmony.

Chapter Three

THE KEY TO NOW!

To accept Divine Guidance, one must surrender their earthly ideas about how things "should be"—and even that is just the beginning! To fully move forward...surrender what surrender looks like!

Living with the Archangelic Realm and receiving the information being revealed reminds us daily to keep surrendering. Accepting the process of Archangelic In-soulment also means that we are on a journey that has recognized, healed, and released many old woundings...and they were not all from this lifetime.

KIRA RAA BEGINS:

As I watched the curved and ceremonially decorated knife descend toward my heart, my eyes were locked with his and my only emotion was pure love... He was truly unaware of the events now set in motion...and the certain destruction that faced all Atlanteans in the very near future.

Was I waking from a dream, or was I still living in it? I am with my dearest beloved and yet *seeing* scenes from what could only be another life together. I had always wondered why there is a peculiar birthmark on my chest that looks like a knife wound scar, yet is irregular. Awareness of this past event began deepening my understanding of the current times. So much had been happening lately, and my mind and my heart were still accepting that everything as I had known it had changed. In a period of only four months, my beloved had appeared, my young children were suddenly and surprisingly no longer living with me, I was bringing forth beings from the Archangelic Realm, leaving old friends, and entering into an entirely new way of life.

What was happening, and how it happened, was beyond any form of a timeline known on this planet. During January 2003, Sri Ram Kaa and I were married...a consecration of our commitment to carry forth the mission that had been so boldly detailed for us just a few months prior.

The power of our blended energies, along with the love and support of those present, merged Earth, Sky, and Spirit to celebrate our Union. We forever opened the pathway that continues to cross all boundaries of dimension, vibration, and understanding. Atlantis seemed so far away, and yet so present!

SRI RAM KAA CONTINUES:

In *Sacred Union: The Journey Home,*[10] we shared the gift of living in Beloved Partnership. Finding your Beloved is a wondrous accomplishment. However, discovering that your Beloved is in body, available, and ready to be in Union with you is an amazing gift!

We are witnessing a phenomenon of more and more spiritually open people finding true partnership. These spiritual couples are finding each other across vast distances. They are listening through the ethers to locate their "other half," for the call to Union is greater now than ever before.

Recently I was chatting with a woman who moved to New Mexico from another state. "What called you here?" I asked. "I came to be with my Beloved," she replied. "Wonderful," I responded. "How is that for you now?" "I feel close," she said. "He's nearby, but I have not met him yet!"

I smiled inwardly, for I knew this woman was correct. Her Beloved partner was indeed nearby, and I admired her courage in taking the steps to make herself available to meet this person.

When Kira and I found each other in 2002, we knew that an important piece of the Mystery of Life had come to its resolution. We felt a profound sense of peace. There was great Joy in feeling the truth of our connection and in knowing that we had a shared mission. What I did not initially understand was that this relationship was a continuation of a marriage that began many millennia ago.

"You have to remember," she said. "We cannot continue until you remember." Kira was entering a clairvoyant trance as she was beginning to start an Angelic In-soulment session. We were alone together in the Arizona desert, during the first days when Zadkiel identified Himself[11] as our Archangelic Messenger. "Remember what?" I responded. Kira seemed very far away as the words, "Remember Atlantis," quietly left her mouth.

I was stunned. For a moment I thought this was some sort of test, that I had to prove I was ready to be with her by demonstrating past-life recall. Could I do this? The first wave of inner reaction to this unexpected request was self-doubt. I looked at Kira and saw how peaceful and relaxed she was. "Just breathe, and connect to our time together in Atlantis," she said.

Taking a couple of deep breaths, I closed my eyes and relaxed. Within moments, I saw my hand rapidly and with great force lowering a knife into the chest of a woman lying before me. There were hundreds of people gathered all around. It was a ceremonial execution.

I gasped loudly as if trying to awaken from a nightmare and exploded, "I killed you!" I was cold, shaking, and in shock. My heart ached and I began to sob. "How could I have done this?" I cried out loud, as tears streamed down my face.

Kira came out of her partial trance and took my hand. "It's OK," she said, offering quiet reassurance. "You had to find this memory yourself so that you could understand what they are about to share with us. You had to connect to the truth of our Atlantean lifetime in order to see how this all fits together."

Still shaking, I could barely speak. "How could I have done that?" The words felt hollow and I kept repeating them, more to myself than out loud. I felt an ancient pain in my heart that had been anchored there for thousands of centuries. I was being asked to reexperience a horrible scene from my past. It was at once painful and healing.

As I connected with the pain, I saw that immediately after I had plunged the knife into Kira's chest, I realized the error of my decision. I recognized that executing her was a grave mistake for all Atlanteans. My pride would not let me reveal this understanding to those who stood at the scene.

When my time in Atlantis ended, I spent many, many lifetimes in other Realms, healing the wound of having rejected my Beloved. There is great support for wounded souls in many Realms of experience. In spite of the great love and acceptance showered upon me, it took much time before I was willing to enter a body and be in a relationship again.

ZADKIEL CAME IN LATER THAT DAY
AND OFFERED GREAT REASSURANCE:

Sri Ram Kaa, you have been separated from the Kira since the end of Atlantis because the power of your Union was too bright to be on the Earth any earlier than now. You have had lifetimes on Earth, but you have never been in body at the same time as Kira, nor have the two of you ever been together since the end time of Atlantis. You were not to reunite until this time of culmination on the planet. You will only be able to fulfill your agreement to reunite if you have fully healed the wound of your Atlantean lifetime.

It was a powerful and universal message: Recognize, remember, and heal, for without healing there cannot be reunion. (I did not realize at that moment that this powerful discernment also had profound global application.) Only then can you move forward in the role you agreed to perform here. It seemed overwhelming to accept the idea that I had been a highly respected person of great power in Atlantis, and that I had used my influence to have my beloved Kira publicly executed.

My mind struggled to resolve these recognitions with the pain that I was still holding in my heart. I felt the abyss of despair that had ensued from my Atlantean lifetime. During the time between lives, there was recognition of what I had done and there was the additional wounding of self-judgment. I experienced the hell that is self-condemnation. I also experienced the fullness of limitless love, as tens of thousands of Angelic energies surrounded me in a cocoon of light, cradling my essence as the wounding subsided.

Such is the mercy and love of the Divine. It is truly our own judgments that create all forms of pain and hell. The universe is always available to heal the separations from love. Centuries passed…

SRI RAM KAA'S VISION, OCTOBER 8, 2002

Sitting on the coffeehouse sofa, relaxing into a morning latte, I felt at peace with the world. Like a daydream, my soft reverie expanded, and an energy stream opened at the back of my head. Noticing the love of this energy, I invited it to come down into my body. My hands felt huge and heavy as if they were growing larger—something bigger than I had entered my space, expanding. Another energy entered my left palm and traveled right up my arm. I accepted this loving presence into me as I felt the purity of the vibration.

I clearly heard: "I am St. Germain. I am here to support you and open you to the truth of your mission and purpose in this time and place. Soon the Earth and its inhabitants will experience a split that some will call ascension, and others will call a dimensional shift. To those left behind, it will be an experience of suffering, pain, and separation."

Lovingly, I was shown a visual of this shift. It was an image of the Earth floating in space with a second Earth simply peeling away from the original image. This higher-frequency Earth separated and lifted from the denser one. From the vantage point of outer space, the one Earth was dark and heavy while the New Earth was lighter and luminous. The lighter one lifted up and away. The space around the darker Earth grew ever darker, as if it were being ushered farther from the Light. I felt into the planet and sensed that its inhabitants were screaming. I was feeling their fear and anger. They were experiencing much suffering.

My emotions came into play. The darkness that surrounded this third-dimensional Earth seemed to be sentencing it to a zone of perpetual suffering. How could there be peace and love if there was not Light? Immediately, I felt sadness and pain.

Relaxing into the experience, I realized the source of my pain. It was tied to the sense that part of myself was still on that planet. I was leaving behind a piece of my heart, and I so wished I could call it back.

My field of awareness then expanded. Through the expansion, I recognized that this darker Earth floats in the endless Ocean of God. In the distance I saw the Earth and the Milky Way as small fragments. They were floating in a sea of consciousness, surrounded by boundless love. From this perspective, I experienced peace.

Each soul that clung to the density of the old Earth had made a choice not to reunite with the boundless Ocean of God. I witnessed the Divine patience, the Infinite Presence of One who unconditionally accepts all creation and all co-creation. Those who clung to the density would continue on a planet of fear and pain until they were complete with that chosen experience. Aligning with the infinite perspective, I knew that at some point these dissonant souls would reunify. It could not be otherwise. Feeling this great trust, I relaxed into a soft expansive Peace as the Presence gently left my body.

Reflecting on the experience, I wrote in my journal: Why should I care? The urgency of this time seems compelling. It is paradoxical to think that we might leave some souls behind. Is that even possible?

I noticed a voice in the distance: *"All must ascend, all are invited, all are needed."* I felt perplexed, and watched as my pen automatically wrote the following lines in my journal:

Oneness is indeed my message. Choice is the responsibility of self-aware Beings. Awareness therefore needs to be invited. Discernment can only be taught if there is a longing for truth. It is the will of the Most High that all be given the opportunity to recognize the choice that greets them.

Each soul is engaged in learning. However, patterns become habits, and the seemingly endless cycle of rebirth and death continues for as long as one chooses. The moment the soul chooses God-consciousness, then the illusion begins to melt. All disease is separation from God. All suffering is a separation. There is one breath that breathes us all.

Prophetic visions, Angelic Communion, and interdimensional sight often accompany spiritual surrender. These phenomena are not required parts of the journey, and often the desire for them interferes with the journey itself. What is universal for all of us on a path of awakening is the need to surrender to the Divine Flow. That is, we must set aside the "It's all about me" orientation, and cultivate loving cooperation with the One Presence and Power.

Surrender deepens as our hearts open. Trust cultivates a willingness to walk into the unknown. Spirit will always provide whatever is truly needed for your spiritual mission. However, Divine timing often reveals a flow that differs from human expectations! Such is the process of living on this side of the veil.

The Visions revealed to Kira and me are not offered as a reward for spiritual discipline. Rather, they have come forward as needed to support our mission of service, and as we had agreed at the end times of Atlantis. They help us find our way.

We share the Visions, as requested by the Archangelic Realm, to help provide context for a better understanding of these times. The information that is imparted often challenges us to further remove ourselves from judgment. It takes practice to integrate new paradigms. The mind does not readily discard its favorite beliefs and world views! Thus, most of us find that we need some integration time and contextual frameworks in order to assimilate new information.

This is the gift of your heart barometer! Throughout this book you will be called to invite your own discernments and integrations. The more you use this valuable tool called the heart instead of the computer-like mind, the greater your experience will be.

THE KEY TO NOW

Energy never dies. Past-life recall offers the opportunity to understand the forces at work in our present experience. Similarly, the tales of Atlantis and Leumeria offer a context for the history of the soul. To receive benefit from that history requires that you set aside your scientific mind and its need for a particular form of proof. Instead, listen to the information and feel what stirs inside.

As you relax into the present moment, you will find the past and the future are blended into the recognition we call "now." As we return to wholeness, the need for linear organizations is released. Time is an artificial unit of separation that removes us from wholeness by distorting our perceptual (mental) lens.

When my vision of the separating planets appeared in Sedona, it was an opportunity to further embrace wholeness by releasing a linear preoccupation. There is no "end of time"; however, there are choices and consequences to all choices. All of our soul experiences have brought us to this time in history. All of them are important.

A CALL TO CLARITY

As we travel the world, sharing the many gifts of the Archangelic Realm, we are often called to present Archangelic In-soulments for very large groups. Often, these groups are filled with people who have neither heard of, nor experienced, the process. Others in attendance are very familiar with traditional channeling, or both channeling and In-soulment.

Without fail, at the end of these loving gatherings, long lines form, tears of recognition and hugs are shared, and occasionally a well-intended soul will declare that we are "not doing it right!" This is then followed by advice on how to *"properly channel,"* according to their best understanding, and opinions as to why Kira is doing it wrong and should not continue. Judgment shrouded in good intentions is often delivered without recognition of the deeper call to clarity.

Why do we share this story with you? Primarily because with each well-intended sharing we are gifted with the choice to continue, the choice to fully place our trust in the Archangelic Realm, in the Presence that is offered through the discourses, and in our own hearts. Yes, the process is unique, yet it is an ancient process, the remembrance of which is simply expanding a modern paradigm. For each who walks away because we are doing it "wrong" in his or her mind, we receive the gift of claiming ever greater trust.

May your Self-trust grow the next time anyone or anything calls you to doubt yourself. When confronted with the declaration that you are doing it wrong, may you call forth that moment as the recognition that if you are in complete trust of the Divine in action, there are no mistakes!

Sri & Kira sharing positive 2012 visions

Chapter Four

A PASSION FOR 2012

From the moment of our reunion, we began regular sessions with Archangel Zadkiel. Every day we would simply sit quietly, turn on the recorder, and welcome our loving messenger. Within weeks, we were quickly inundated with volumes of information. We felt overwhelmed at the task of how to disseminate it all properly. Kira Raa and I knew that our mission was to live the work, not to simply offer words. Our routine of prayer and communion increased as the Divine information flowed into our consciousness.

Recognizing the importance of the information and eager to share, we began appearing at New Age expos, bookstores, and conferences. It was challenging to begin sharing publicly, risking judgment and confrontation, and Kira Raa was timid about bringing Archangel Zadkiel through during our first public appearances, for in doing so she would be quite vulnerable and open. We learned with practice that we were energetically shielded and that even the hearts of the greatest skeptics opened when they felt the radiance of pure love. Together we began to relax and trust more deeply.

We diligently continued our work and experienced many physical changes as a result of our diet and spiritual alignments. In June 2004, Archangel Zadkiel announced that we would be entering into a 40-day fast from the middle of July until September. We were terrified and stunned! How could we possibly go 40 days without food? We had already experienced a 10-day fast several times, and this felt most complete. The idea of 40 days seemed daunting at first. What was missing, and why did we have to do this?

Our questions were all answered with loving support, guidance, and reassurance as to why the request was made, and as with all requests, we were reminded that we had the option of saying no. Yet, the closer we came to the "start date," the more it became apparent that this would, indeed, offer us a great shift in energy and open the doorway to even greater world service.

The 40-day fast was an amazing journey. Daily we would thank the universe for bringing us to TOSA ranch. It was the perfect setting to maximize the sacredness and gifts being showered upon us. With each passing day we became ever more aware of the greater energies that are present for all Beings.

Our conscious communion with Source deepened and new information was seeded in us. We learned to pull energy from the sun[12] and the air. Hunger was never an issue and our vitality was astonishing. By the end of the fast, our only fear was the return to eating!

Honoring the many gifts of the fast would be a book in itself! Suffice it to say, we integrated many new lessons, energies, and understandings. Most gloriously, we were freed from many limiting beliefs, including those that challenged even our most open minds. We discovered, at a basic cellular level, that food is optional, and that death is truly an illusion. To know these truths at our core offered great freedom.

Archangel Zadkiel announced to us that it was time to start sharing His messages with the public, and we thus began inviting friends to gather together in October 2004. The Lotus Temple at TOSA ranch became the perfect setting to offer these messages, which became a monthly event. The birth of the public discourses was upon us, and our passion to bring forth all of the information being gifted to the world was amplified.

Sri & Kira at the October, 2004 first monthly gathering

We invited a few friends familiar with our work to attend the first discourse and were delighted to have many others who'd simply "heard about it" show up that last Saturday in October. Without any formal announcements, we had a full house! The loving clarity of the Archangelic Presence had revealed, yet again, the gift of simply trusting. Sharing this monthly gathering as a community of friends has been diligently continued since that first Saturday.

When the monthly gatherings began, we were unaware that they would catalyze the dissemination of material in a manner that would quickly reach around the world. We began posting transcriptions of the messages at our website,[13] attracting subscribers from all over the world who wanted to receive the Archangelic discourses each month. With the assistance of our loving TOSA Angels, these messages are transcribed and available free of charge for all to enjoy and study.

To our great delight, each day we receive many letters from our newsletter subscribers, for the Archangelic energies and information are touching many lives in such a good way. We trust that each person who reads the messages will be invited into ever-greater clarity and trust in their own path as we all continue preparing for the times just ahead.

As beings of Light, we all have the wondrous opportunity to be freshly aware and in awe of the many gifts showered upon us at any given time. Such are the gifts we embrace daily through living at TOSA and experiencing the presences of the Archangels through In-soulment.

Living with these energies can be initially taxing on a system that has been navigating density for quite some time. We reflect fondly on those well-intentioned friends who cautioned us just before our 40-day fast, "You can't do that; you are no longer 33 years old!"

So true, and yet, one of the many benefits we are experiencing is the process of reverse-aging. We are also delighted to witness this among many of those who visit us each month. The gifts of the many practices from the Archangelic Realm have greatly accelerated this process. They are a form of yoga, and together constitute the Galactic Yogic traditions which were utilized during the Atlantean experience.

The Lotus Temple at TOSA ranch, NM

We offer you some of these practices for reflection and connection throughout the chapters of this book. All of these practices will open your energy field. They will make it easier for you to navigate the increasing polarity and fear on our planet with greater personal clarity. Regardless of your spiritual orientation, these practices will expand your energy.

They feel great and are simple to do. You are encouraged to fully read the practice as it is explained, and then to offer yourself a moment to put down the book and actually experience it in its fullness. If you are so inclined, you may even wish to start a journal about your experiences with these practices.

THE 2012 CONVERSATION

Through our extensive interactions with the Archangelic Realm, we have also been gifted with extensive information from the Ascended Masters, and others of great benevolent energy. These experiences have offered us a more ascended perspective toward events on Earth. This process has expanded our own recognition that this moment in our linear timeline on this planet is indeed a portal of communication that extends well beyond this Earth.

Running through our many conversations is a consistent theme of reassurance, preparation, and noninterference. The messages always invite us to trust our own hearts and reconnect with our higher wisdom. Often we are reminded that ALL of the numerous messages being showered upon our planet at this time come by invitation. That is, the Angels remind us that we invited them to appear at this time in our collective history to help us remember.

Yet, when did this conversation really begin? Or has it ever ended? Perhaps, similar to Kira Raa, you were born clairvoyant. Commonly, many have the gift of intuition and may call it something else, yet there is a deep recognition or intuitive presence that may have called to you in one way or another during your lifetime. We often hear stories of the mother who hears her child calling, yet no words were uttered, or the child who knew when his parent in a distant land was dying, etc. These are not coincidences; they are gentle reminders of the deeper resonance each of us is capable of connecting with.

You may have had a dream that has come true, or one that served as forewarning to prevent a disaster. These experiences are numerous and have been documented throughout our human history. Similarly, so is the 2012 conversation, only unlike any other time in our history, we are here…now!

When Kira Raa was just a young child (only five years old), she was gifted with a prophetic vision of the world in 2012. This vision left her frightened and seeking answers. Following the vision, an answer came in the form of "the most loving and gentle voice I have ever heard"; she heard the words: *And this is just one option for your world.* " The fact that the future was open to influence fueled her unending energy and passion to share with as many people as possible that there are many options for this time in history.

A teenager in the sixties and fully aware of world events around him, Sri Ram Kaa has always been on the journey of self-discovery. From an early age he recognized that our world was being prepared for a monumental shift. Through a decades-long journey that included numerous religions, spiritual leaders, psychotherapy, and self-help techniques, he arrived at the certainty that our soul is "the One" we have been looking for.

Together, we are passionate about the 2012 conversation. Our passion transcends the dogma of many established prophecies, and this book is a journey to your own discovery of what, in the end, 2012 will bring to you, to our planet, and to our universe. The future is not yet written "in stone;" however, trends are in place.

May your passion be ignited as you read on, and may your heart expand through the practices offered as a balance to the information that your brain seeks to put to rest about these times.

CHOOSING A SPIRITUAL LIFE
IN A TECHNOLOGICALLY DRIVEN TIME

Spirituality is not religion. It is the essential inner knowing that the force that animates life is not of the flesh; it is within the flesh and permeates all matter. Our Spiritual Knowing is an intuitive quality that recognizes love expressing through a variety of forms. It is the same quality that finds meaning and inspiration in beauty.

Spiritual wisdom results from spiritual communion. Mankind had a more direct communion with the unseen intelligence in earlier times, when man lived closer to nature. Yet nature is not the sole source of such knowledge; it is more accurately a gateway. The natural world is a doorway to an Authenticity that opens the human awareness and makes it more available to the fullness of "what is." Consciousness itself is fluid, expansive, and all-inclusive. The content of consciousness is that an object or perception has a form or boundary; however, consciousness itself is endless. Thus, our brain limits our perceptions to fix a context for meaning. We relate to the content, not the field of interaction. Modern society has generated fields of stimulation that keep the brain so occupied with content, that the spaciousness of consciousness is lost.

The modern city-dweller is bombarded by noise, smells, visual advertising, music, chatter, and cell phone conversations. How many people do you notice who have an earpiece fastened to their heads? Cell phones command one's attention. It is alarming how overstimulated modern man has become. Alarming, simply because in the overwhelming din one loses the continuity of flow, the spaciousness of the field of awareness that opens the doors of understanding and trust.

People who meditate in any manner report that their meditation practice becomes a sanctuary, a beautiful communion with spaciousness that offers a peaceful respite from the world, one that nourishes them with essential reassurance. Meditation connects one to the essential. From this connection we gain soul refreshment, a sense of reassurance and aliveness that is beyond the emotions.

Living a spiritual life requires that we cultivate a sense of connection with the Greater Flow. Whether that connection is cultivated through sitting meditation, gardening, painting, or music, matters not. Many people can enter the connective consciousness through walking, dancing, Tai Chi, or other forms of movement. Spiritual connection is not something one strives for to cope with modern life; it is who you are! The purpose of spiritual practice is to keep your consciousness actively connected to this truth.

The world is filled with opportunities and enticements to disconnect. Yet this is actually a gift, for when one disconnects from the essential, one can gain discernment regarding one's own connection. Remaining disconnected for long periods will result in many different forms of illness. The body requires connection to the essential rhythms and harmony of the natural world to operate properly. When your consciousness remains disconnected from these natural rhythms, the body reacts with pain or symptoms. Instead of simply seeking medication for the pain, we suggest you first take a deep breath and detach from the experience by saying "thank you" to the body for reminding you that you have been forcing an unnatural expectation upon it! It is easy to stay healthy if you remain consciously connected.

Connection to the Greater Flow also nourishes the soul. The soul animates the body. In fact, the soul is in a most sacred and respectful union with the body. Thus, often our bodies will know things before our conscious mind discovers them. A felt sense in the body, such as gooseflesh or a tight stomach, can be the signal to consciousness that an energy has shifted. The body can signal a change in energy in a variety of ways. As you begin to pay attention to these signals, conscious communion with your body is enhanced. This builds even greater trust, respect, and self-empowerment. You have been given a great gift!

IS RELIGION SPIRITUALITY?

Most of the world's great faiths have a founding prophet. These inspired Beings became illuminated with Truth and shared a teaching with those around them. While the teachings have varied from culture to culture, each Teacher pointed the way to Oneness, a way to the dissolution of earthly pains and into a heavenly bliss. Each Teacher offered words and practices designed to support spiritual unfoldment. Whether reunion with the Father, an idyllic heaven, or the stillness of Nirvana, the goal was one of release from the individual's suffering.

Over the centuries their teachings became formalized, the stories shifted, and the teachings were necessarily distorted and modified to be understood within various cultural contexts. Whenever interpretations are added to a teaching, those interpretations carry a context. Thus, the context of a moment in time, a culture, a level of education, a bias, etc.—all color the original teaching. Over many centuries the teachings can indeed become a blended body of work. Thus, religion becomes veiled, and one must look beyond the symbols, practices, and histories that cloak the original lessons of Light.

Religion is born after a spiritual calling is felt; it provides the spiritual seeker with codes, teachings, community, etc. Religion offers social order and a pathway for teaching the ego-self how to cooperate in a social context. It is a useful institution that brings order to society.

Ultimately, religion hopes to conform its members to a common stream of consciousness and thus, over time, organized religions have sought to protect their identities by finding fault in those who were nonconforming, or who conformed to "opposing" system. World religions have become differentiated expressions of the Universal Spirit that have a self-preserving interest based upon their unique offerings and differences from other faiths. Thus, religious wars have brought suffering to many over the ages. Fighting "in the name of God" is a rallying call to inspire men to go to battle, regardless of whether God ordered men to battle!

The minds and earthly motives of human beings have infiltrated the spiritual purity of many religious practices and policies. So it is with all earthly institutions. Thus, ultimately, it is up to the individual to shift and filter out dogma from living truth. Even though you may want advice or guidance from an outside authority, whether you accept that guidance and how you act upon it is up to you. It always comes back to you and your willingness to commit your life energy to a belief and/or an action.

Recognize that you are already a mystic! Whether you notice it or not, you are relying upon your inner Self in every moment. It is you who decides to follow your doctor's advice. It is you who decides to conform to your peers' expectations, or listen to the latest expert. While you might be relying upon an expert, ultimately the choice to conform is yours. Life will offer you feedback on your choices. If your life has pain, then those outside experts you have consulted are simply disconnected from what is right for you. Pain is nature's signal that we have lost connection with our Authentic Self. Our Authentic Self knows exactly what we need in any moment. We have simply lost the art of listening. This is the essence of living a spiritual life...listening, and being present to our essential connection.

Everyone is spiritual, BUT not everyone is awake to their spirituality. That is, spirituality is inseparable from Life. Whether you recognize and develop your spiritual senses is a choice. Spiritual recognition offers the glue that connects seemingly separate persons with a common bond. It also connects all living beings and seemingly insentient thing.

THE SCIENCE OF SPIRITUALITY

A felt sense, an intuitive knowing, is easily dismissed by the mind. Our world has conditioned the mind to prefer and place its faith in solid data. As we really start to look deeper, however, we discover that there is a science of spirituality. There are many spiritual disciplines. The oldest (that we know of) were developed in the East. The inner journey has been well documented by these spiritual sojourners. The huge popularity of yoga in Western cultures is a testament to Western man's desire to cultivate spiritual consciousness. Without it, life is experienced as a disconnected collection of thoughts, feelings, and events.

Choosing spirituality means choosing to look beyond the surface and to trust the subtle senses. It also means listening deeply to one's heart, for the heart is the gateway to the soul. This can be a big leap for some people...and it is a journey that must be made if your life is to find its deepest meaning and value. Choosing a spiritual life also means that you will trust an unseen energy for guidance. No longer will the mind alone be called upon to make your decisions. No longer will your life be steered solely by authorities and conventional wisdom—your actions will be qualified by your heart's knowing.

This simple yet challenging shift brings great peace to you. The heart opens the gateway to the Peace that transcends all understanding and indeed opens the doorway to the universal, a mystical realm that connects your individuated expression with All that Is. Such is the treasure! Yet, modern technological society fears the independence and personal autonomy that comes with direct connection to Divine Wisdom. Why is this? Because it results in the redistribution of power, thereby creating a new sense of being. Power is no longer found in the outer world.

For millennia, mankind could focus on the outer world and dance in time to polarity and dualistic mindsets. For millennia, we trod on the Earth seeking survival, and only when our bellies were full did we consider the arts and spiritual pursuits. Times have changed. Mankind is out of balance with the Earth. Mankind is out of balance with the Inner Essence. The Earth's inhabitants are being given a spiritual wake-up call. Are you listening?

There is an urgent call to refocus. Priorities must shift. Actually, this dawning recognition of the One True Power will not collapse society—it will cause people to take more responsibility for one another. Instead of blaming their politicians, people will show up and offer help and innovative ideas. The mind finds differences while the heart finds commonality. The mind seeks to identify and "deal with" problems, while the heart finds the strength to move forward to a workable solution.

We have the technology to destroy the world. In fact, our addiction to fossil-fuel technologies has already destroyed much of our planet. We have the ability to use technology to further separate from our hearts and souls. We also have the ability to make technology our servant, not our master.

What does this mean? It means reclaiming proper priorities within ourselves. As we choose wholeness and heart-centered balance in our personal consciousness, our world will shift to reflect this new inner balance. Heart-based action is inherently moral; it is universal and loving. It is the energetic foundation for a Golden Age.

Chapter Five

THE HOLY WAR HAS BEGUN

THE WORLD IS ACTING OUT!

There is a tendency in human beings to deny or avoid change. While a Sunday drive into the countryside may be felt as refreshing, a hard look at oneself is usually resisted. It's a cliché to say that people are creatures of habit…yet indeed we are.

Sitting as a psychotherapist taught Sri Ram Kaa that the obvious is often overlooked, and that incomplete solutions are often applied to fairly simple problems. For example, when a child begins acting out in school and displaying defiant behavior, an opportunity presents itself for the entire family to come together and unify in support of resolution. The mother and father can both find common ground in their love for the child, and together seek solutions to stabilize the home environment in an effort to meet the child's needs. At least that's one approach that offers holistic, comprehensive support.

47

An alternative approach might be to send the child to boarding school. If the parents are unwilling to look deeply at the family dynamics, then they are simply removing the child from the environment where the problem occurs and letting the new school assume responsibility as guardian. This is mere delegation and never truly addresses the deeper issues, the unexpressed emotions, unmet needs, or health conditions underpinning the child's behavior. Yet it often seems to work. In the new environment, the child may find new ways of coping, and the parents are not challenged to change themselves.

How does this relate to 2012, you might ask? Quite simply, our world is "acting out"—there is increased war, social unrest, weakening economic stability and frustration with the "powers that be." Many, reacting to their loss of stability, have sought fundamentalist approaches, hoping that a rigid approach to morality will offer them the reassuringly safe structures they no longer find in the outer world.

Yes, a child who "acts out" needs boundaries and guidance. However, the call for boundaries is really a call for safety. Defiant children are really asking, "Am I safe?" and "Do you love me?" Boundaries offer a sense of safety and support if accompanied by loving wisdom. However, whenever dysfunctional behavior occurs, the one "acting out" needs something more than the traditional approach of punishment or a "time out." What is also needed is reassurance, loving redirection, and a listening ear from the parent. All dysfunction can be healed through loving attention to the essential needs that the "culprit" is failing to express in a healthy manner. Dysfunctional behavior results when one is unaware of his or her true needs. Thus, by listening with loving wisdom, and looking deeply, we can discover what is truly needed. The child (or adult!) feels respected during the process. This is healing.

So…humanity is acting out. People are strapping bombs to their chests and killing other human beings as they kill themselves. Is this not similar to the child who rebels in school, or the one who cuts himself or takes drugs? There is no boarding school where we can send the terrorists. Instead, we seek to erect barriers around them in an effort to protect ourselves. Yet the barriers have been placed with anger and the energy of domination. No guidance or redirection is offered. No healing is offered. Thus, the parents of the terrorists, and the terrorists themselves, keep rearing more dysfunctional children…who don't really know how to correct themselves. They are victims of a cycle that is fueled by the lack of loving attention from those who have the power to intervene. Without loving guidance and sincere concern for their wellbeing, the behavior will not stop. Terrorism is a natural expression of a belief system that sees no exit from its outrage and pain.

The terrorism issue is only one of many facing humanity. It serves to remind us that human beings have universal needs. That all residents of planet Earth share a common human heart. Each human being needs community, a basic trust in life itself, and a sense of self-respect. Each needs to believe they have the power of choice. If we look past the window dressing of race and culture, we will find the universal language of the human soul. Why then do we fear each other?

Many people fear terrorism, gang violence, and drug-related crime. In their fear they are anchoring a belief that they themselves are powerless. This belief finds expression as anger and force. Anger is a seemingly empowering emotion that expresses itself through forceful action. Anger may make the victim feel stronger, but it does not heal the relationship with the feared person/persons.

In Western society and other areas of the world, responsibility for environmental, social, healthcare, and educational needs has been delegated to the elected government officials. The political structures, heavily influenced by special interests and frequently funded by Big Business, have lost sight of their primary purpose for being—to serve the people. Instead, people are seen as voters who must be mesmerized by hope and fear during election years so that the agendas of corporate special interests can move forward. An oversimplification, perhaps. However, that special interests have been woven into every department of government is now self-evident. And even with these special interests within every governmental department, there are still people who sincerely want to serve their constituents. Often their hands are tied.

For example, in the United States, war is big business; it generates huge profits for bankers and military contractors. The profits are so large that these corporations see human lives as "acceptable losses" and have completely lost touch with the essential human spirit. War becomes an agenda that offers an outlet for the fear and anger of an uneducated populace.

The citizens have handed over responsibility for their country's resources to a political system that has become more corrupt and disconnected from true wisdom with each passing year. Like giving power to an adolescent, the result is a system that addresses only short-term wants and desires. The system cannot heal itself, for it is caught in a destructive paradigm. Like an addict who must live from "fix to fix," the machinery of government cannot buy its way out of the problem. Caught in a web of corporate interests, and needing to keep the general population ignorant and appeased, the political system has prioritized its survival over its quality of service. It has sold out in many ways. No amount of money or power heals a destructive value system. Personal change within such a system comes only when its very survival is threatened. Because the delegated government is so far removed from its higher wisdom and the hearts of its constituents, no change will ever occur through talk or petition. As Einstein put it, "No problem can be solved from the same level of consciousness that created it."

To effect true change, the government's level of consciousness must rise. Hoping that this change in consciousness will happen spontaneously is like expecting that an addict might voluntarily give up his next fix. It is unlikely that our government will evolve unless its very survival is threatened. Government mirrors human emotions and ego; therefore, change is more likely if it hits bottom, whether through collapse of the economy, environmental catastrophe, or an uprising of the people. However, we are not advocating or eager for any of the above; instead, we see that if the population lifts its consciousness, if enough people bring universal spiritual values to the forefront, then the politicians will follow that lead. In short, it is unrealistic to expect the government to be the leader. After all, government was created to be the servant.

Change will be resisted till the bitter end by those who fear the loss of power or respect if such change is embraced. For example, it was known for decades that cigarettes are extremely deleterious to human health. Yet many politicians, physicians, and corporations continued to deny the evidence until public opinion and the more enlightened medical community came together. Once it became popular to support public nonsmoking, the politicians jumped on board. But not until the scientific studies were overwhelmingly conclusive could such an action be considered safe for their careers. Most would not assume a leadership role in changing the face of social behavior or in safeguarding health if it meant losing corporate support or public approval. Rather than educate their constituents about the wisdom of a change, our "leaders" simply pander to voters, pacify their special-interest groups, and seek continued power and job security. When public opinion changes, then the politicians are sure to follow.

Let this be a reminder that you have the power to change the world by living the change in your own heart. As Gandhi advised, "Be the change you wish to see in the world."

Former Vice President Al Gore has been championing public awareness of the impact of modern life on the environment. The changes in the Arctic ice pack are happening so fast, and are so alarming that scientists worldwide are uniting around the truth that we have severely damaged our environment. So what are our governments doing about it? Very little.

Just as cigarettes' connection to lung cancer was evaded for decades, once again corporate profits are being sheltered at the expense of our shared environment. Know that our purpose in underscoring these issues is not to enjoin you to join an activist group, or to vote for some favored candidate. We consider these issues to illustrate a point about human psychology.

You see, the decision has already been made. Government will not take widespread action until the public screams. Global warming has been ignored too long and now drastic and expensive decisions must be made if catastrophe is to be avoided. Imagine the world's oceans rising just two feet in the coming decade. That is what current science predicts. The impact on every seaport and low-lying area across the globe would be huge, and flooding would be experienced on every continent. Factor in some earthquakes and storms, courtesy of our changing weather patterns, and lowlands everywhere are sure to be affected.[14]

Our intent in sharing this is not to scare you. We are inviting you to wake up. Sometimes the truth is shocking when we've had our attention elsewhere. Action could be taken in a methodical and planned manner right now. Instead, government keeps our collective eye on terrorism and rising gasoline prices. These issues not only serve private interests, they keep the public in fear. And a fearful populace is much easier to control than a society of empowered thinkers.

The deck is stacked toward further chaos and instability, so how will you respond? The time is *now* for personal reflection and proactive actions. As humanity finds its collective heart and releases the grip of fear upon its consciousness, we can indeed develop creative solutions to every condition we observe. The human spirit, when inspired, is capable of resolving any challenge it faces. There is no problem on this planet that can not be solved through intelligent and selfless action. The first step is to move out of fear and anchor our energy in self-trust.

Smart people do dumb things! It doesn't take intelligence to make healthy changes; it takes self-trust. It takes action. The courage to unhook from a destructive paradigm and embrace a healthier perspective does not come without some feelings of instability. All change is felt as instability at first. Foundational change is usually fought, not embraced. It is frightening to anyone to recognize that the beliefs they invested so much of their identity in no longer serve. Each human being contributes to the problem or to the solution. What does it take to cultivate new habits? We must trust ourselves enough to tolerate the temporary instability while taking committed action.

Perhaps the Holy War is, in fact, the competition for your attention. That is, if your attention is distracted by worldly preoccupations and fear, then you will perpetuate the established trends. That is exactly where mass consciousness is presently focused. However, if your attention recognizes that fear and self-doubt are empowering destructive trends, then you can make new choices. A heart-centered perspective is holistic and wise; it will find a way to meet everyone's needs. So how do we make the transition?

Chapter Six

RECONNECTING WITH AUTHENTIC SOUL KNOWING

One of the questions that we frequently hear is, "How does one interpret these Archangelic messages?" Archangel Zadkiel has brought clarity to the interpretation of these messages as we all embrace the gift of being a Conscious Decision Maker.

Many of the messages and practices in this book originated from the monthly discourses held at TOSA ranch, our home in New Mexico. They represent a consistent outpouring of love and reassurance from the Archangelic Realm, often serving as a springboard for further questions.

Conscious Co-creation

~Archangel Zadkiel

The purpose of receiving Angelic Communication is so that one may have an opportunity to first remember and reconnect with their Authentic Soul knowing.

In the reconnection, in the knowing, and in the being-ness of your Authentic Soul, all decisions are readily apparent. They come from a center of love that can only be expressed from the soul level. It is not the illusionary love that has conditions, boundaries and judgments. It is the love that goes beyond self-service, and the love that says, "I see with clarity; therefore, I am able to be a conscious co-creator."

When one is in the presence of a direct Angelic Communication (Insoulment), it provides the opportunity to remember and re-connect with choice. Understand that an opportunity is just that; it is the making available of a choice. Once in the availability of the choice, one immediately connects with the energy, or one immediately repels it.

There are those who will read a message and immediately feel their heart center open, who immediately feel a rush of warm love, who understand deep connectivity. There are also those to whom the message offers the great gift of affirmation to remain in density. They are the ones who make the choice to repel. It is important to recognize that this too is a great gift! It is wonderful that they are in the presence of the energy to affirm their path, no matter what it is. For each path is perfect, all six billion on this planet. Do you understand?

SRI RAM KAA: Yes, and what you appear to be suggesting is that it will be helpful for people to understand the role and the presence of the Angelic Communicator.

Yes! It brings them to the next step, the next choice. First, they have the opportunity for connection, to open up and to go into their heart-soul center. Then, the information that is offered provides the opportunity to make a conscious decision.

A conscious decision is unlike a decision that is made from obligation, from habit, or from condition. A conscious decision is one that comes from pure love, and creates pure service for the greater whole. It is a decision that one can only make when first in the presence of unconditional love and authenticity. For then the information provided is not prophecy, is not prediction.

These are simply words (prophecy and prediction). They are words that are offered by many to intrigue. Words that are offered to give someone an egoic presence, an egoic understanding—my ego wants drama, my ego wishes to participate. This is not what an Angelic Communication is.

Angelic Communication of the purest level offers Divine, Universal information. This communication meets with your Divine Source, providing the opportunity for you to be a Conscious Decision Maker.

Now that one has the information, then one has the opportunity to participate in a conscious decision as a means to respond. There is always a response available for each individual path. All responses originating from an unconditional love center are made whole. This means that each will have their own interpretation of the message based upon their own path and consciousness.

It is important for each individual to take in the information and understand through their own heart-center what that message means for them. Each message is different.

Should anyone try to interpret a message for another, then it is their path they are offering, which limits the interpretation.

To love all six billion, to be present with all on this planet and others, one must be in complete harmony with their own unique understanding of Divine recognition.

As messengers, we simply offer the message. What each does with the message is the choice of their own Divine guidance.

As humanity is moving forward at our point in collective history, there are many powerful choices ahead, and many choices that have already influenced our existence. Without the development of our own inner communication with our soul, we can be swayed by outside influences. Outside influences are projections of other people's ego-needs. They do not lead us to deep peace and enlightenment!

For example, let's return for a moment to the prophecies of Nostradamus. Many readers are committed to the extreme and dramatic interpretation of the quatrains based upon the "proof" of those that appear to have already played out. For example, the famous quatrain in which many believe that Nostradamus saw and even named Hitler. This is an important moment to stop and pay attention.

Yes, World War II happened, and yes, so did Hitler. However, perhaps we are actually revisiting a chicken/egg scenario. What if the "proof" of Nostradamus's quatrains comes from the years of prophetic information, residing in our collective consciousness? What if the manifestation of the drama is more hindsight than foresight?

We ask this sincerely, for if indeed history repeats itself, then perhaps the purpose of this prophecy is to assist us in waking up prior to another catastrophic event.

Atlantis ended in a dramatic fashion. How we chose to end Atlantis, and the choices that have been made collectively throughout our existence, are before us again. The information from the Atlantean times is not readily accessed with clarity, for it involves thinning the veil that separates us from recollection of our past lives. Making wise choices is very important, and having the past as a context is helpful. However, preoccupation with past lives can be a distraction from simply listening to your heart. It can also entice you into revisiting energies that are not for this time, and are thus a trap. When we remember that our heart carries the wisdom gained through all of our past lives, we free ourselves to be fully present for this one without any baggage!

Accepting ourselves as Conscious Decision Makers is not an easy task. The purest essence of the Conscious Decision Maker reveals that through our consciousness, we align with full responsibility for not only our day-to-day actions on this planet, but for *ALL* actions, past, present, and future.

The acceptance of full responsibility for our actions is both liberating and troubling to the egoic shell that wishes to control.[15] It is then that you open to the recognition that Consciousness is a Symptom of the soul! We offer the word "symptom," so that as with all physical symptoms, once the manifestation appears, your attention becomes present to the solution. Delight in recognizing that through the choice to be a Conscious Decision Maker, you indeed validate the presence of the soul via the symptom.

YOUR SOUL IS CONSCIOUSNESS, AND IT IS CONSCIOUS!

Many have prophesied about this time in our collective history, and many have been polarized, according to their beliefs. Some seek the Rapture, some seek war, others seek Nirvana, and many just hope the status quo will continue! By embracing the truth that all six billion are sparks of the Divine, and all six billion paths are perfect, it becomes evident that each person will experience these culminating times in whichever manner they choose to call forth. Archangel Zadkiel expressed insights about this in the following passage:

It is the time of the recognition of the great love of the Oneness. It is the time for all to come home. It is the time for all to recognize. Sri Ram Kaa, when we say the all, it is all those who are ready, all those who have agreed to be present at this time.

SRI RAM KAA: When you say "present," are you referring to all those who are occupying vessels?

Yes, present for Self-Ascension in the way that we are teaching you. So let me clarify. Of the six billion, who are all going home, there are those who have agreed to go home in a less volatile manner, in a less traumatic manner than others. For those, it is their time to activate the love that they are.

SRI RAM KAA: So another way to say that, is those who are present to Self-Ascension are being activated?

Yes.

SRI RAM KAA: And those who are not present to that, those who are so invested in the external world?

We love. We love even deeper. Love them ever more because they are not responsible at this time. Love them because they are not aware of the repeat; they are not aware that they have done this all before. They are unable to consciously co-create the remainder.

SRI RAM KAA: Is our role to offer an opportunity for activation, or is it to activate?

57

Perhaps both. As a conscious co-creator your mission is to listen, to love, and to provide the space for enlightenment. That will create both, Sri Ram Kaa.

SRI RAM KAA: Yes, like sunshine on a seedling.

Yes. Listen, love, and hold the space for enlightenment. Listen, love, be enlightenment. Embody your mission rather than see it as being an outside vehicle. Recognize it is you. You shall have greater Light definition and greater Light frequency that will inspire even more. Listen, love, enlighten. This is what you are. This is the who that you are.

And so it is for all of us...There are no victims on this planet! Each is a co-creator, yet few are *conscious* co-creators. Regardless of their awareness, each person is aligning with the experience he or she wishes to have at this time.

We exist in a "free-will zone," and everyone on Earth gets to have what they want. Having what you want is an energetic experience, and not necessarily an outward expression. Trends have already been set in motion. As you become more aware, you can make new and better-informed choices. In the coming chapters we will explore the question, "What do I want?" and offer practices to assist in calling this forward from your Divine consciousness, freed from the mind.

Resolution appears in understanding the soul as *conscious consciousness—that is, consciousness aware of itself.* From this one discernment, the clarifying recognition of the eternal soul becomes apparent. Collectively, as eternal souls, we are at a time of great reunification, and the choice is upon us to decide how to continue.

CHILDREN OF THE ILLUSION

The Angels and Ascended Ones often refer to us as "dear children"—what is the meaning of this? It is more than a term of endearment. The Angelic Guides who come to assist in our awakening offer unconditional loving energy, like healthy parental mentors. Calling us their children is indeed a term of endearment; however, there is a deeper meaning. Returning to a healthy relationship with the ego requires that we treat it like the child it is. Now is the time to be loving and accepting, to offer guidance (not condemnation) to the ego. The popularity of "Inner Child" therapy is actually an effort to honor and heal the ego. Try to remember that the ego is not your wise soul; it is a vehicle that comes with the body, a support system, not a controlling one.

Everyone who takes birth on Earth acquires an ego. Thus, all humans are like children, living in a childhood fantasy. It is charming when a four-year-old talks about the Easter Bunny or Santa Claus, is it not? Our density concepts about aliens, religion, God, and man are similar delusions. Just as a child cannot conceive of realities outside the ideas he trusts, so too mankind cannot awaken to expanding paradigms without increased trust.

Trust empowers maturity and growth. Alignment with our deepest connection cultivates greater trust and knowledge. Truth is not a concept to be learned. Truth is the remembering that comes with the capacity to integrate its energy. Without this capacity cultivated in one's consciousness, a person cannot "believe," for they cannot yet integrate the information.

Children we are! Awakening we are! Celebrate the unfolding expansion. Dance, laugh, and delight for all. Allow those who slumber to enjoy their rest. Soon enough they will be conscious of their truth.

THE ATLANTEAN END TIMES SPEAK

When we momentarily allow the absolute recognition of the eternal soul, memories of the Atlantis experience become an integral piece in comprehending our planet now. It provides an understanding of ourselves as beings of Light, and the Divine Energy of Love that has many names and expressions. Embracing our being as a Conscious Decision Maker, we then move forward with greater recognition of the importance of the one as part of the whole.

Atlantis was a time of experience with many similarities to Earth, an advanced civilization that evolved in full recognition of its galactic inheritance. The spiritual nature of mankind was understood. There was connection to other worlds and realms of existence. Yet, although the

Atlantean world began with a more enlightened connection, a thinner veil, and greater conscious understanding than found on Earth, Atlantis ended in decay and disaster. Archangel Zadkiel offers a glimpse of the Atlantean world and teaches about conscious decision-making in the following discourse.

Good Day. What does one mean when one says "Good day?" Is one say-ing, "I desire you to have good day?" Is one saying that it is a good day, and is it not a judgment as to what a good day is? We simply offer you this analogy to have some fun, and to remember that joy is deep centered knowing-ness. The concept of good and bad is judgmental, is it not? Per-haps it should be Joyous day.

Sri Ram Kaa: Gratitude day.

Yes, or simply Namaste. I see the Divine in you as you see the Divine in me; is this not a most blessed greeting? It is simply a greeting that says holy one to holy one. For is not each one a holy one? It is a declaration, and it has no doing-ness assigned to it.

Know that it is the sense of doing-ness that creates the stress-filled world, the sense of completing tasks according to the false god of time and schedule. This creates the illusion of pressure, of non-completion. As an authentic being you are already complete. You are already complete-ness, and you have already brought yourself to the gift of completion through your many experiences. Remember this: It is most important to understand that you are complete.

Complete-ness is a most appropriate description for these times. Your planet has long been blanketed by many illusions, or veils. When you thin the veil by opening to greater possibilities and expanding your understanding, all becomes visible. When you remove the veil, that which we call the illusion is no longer available to be seen, and all becomes Oneness. This is how you know the veil is still here. It is appropriate and perfect that the veil is here or you would not be able to continue being in this illusion in the form of a body.

Some would claim it to be a miracle for one to be here and fully released of the illusion. One would be in a state of what you would call suspended animation yet able to maintain communication. Comprehend for a moment what this may look like or could be like, for in both an indirect and direct way it is indeed the state of the planet.

The planet is in suspended animation now. It is in the suspended animation of the illusion. Here, yet not here, and able to communicate. This is a powerful understanding as you approach the Quantum Leap in consciousness. You seek to understand the energetic shifting, and you seek to understand what is happening at this time on the planet. We understand your searching and this is why we respond. We are present to respond and to offer you greater insight and depth.

You have collectively entered a phase from which there can be no turning back. Many new energies are now focused toward your planet as your ability to fully release the illusion increases.

These energetic pulls on your planet will cause what many will call tragedies. Weather that will be quite severe and not seen in a long time, great cataclysms of the Earth and rapid escalation of polarities will escalate war and drama. We wish not to dwell here; we simply wish to offer you this knowing as a means of preparation.

In this escalation there is also the time for the greatest and fastest escalation of the work of joy. This is the gift you are being given during this time. Take advantage of this gift, for you are in the wave now; allow the escalation of the joy to be.

Speak your truth; do not hold back when asked. Hold space, listen, and love, yet respond to those who sincerely inquire. Pay attention to opportunities that are coming your way, pay attention to those who seek you out. Be not afraid to speak.

As your world moves ever more into fear, safety will be sought in many ways. It is imperative to hold the space of true safety, that which comes from within.

Know that safety can only be found when you are able to clearly view the illusion without participating in it.

Re-define relationship as the soul-centered ecstasy of joyously celebrating the truth. Be free of illusion so that you may embrace the knowing of the truth of your being-ness. This is relationship.

SRI RAM KAA: True relationship begins with knowing who you are.

All relationship begins in the ecstatic knowingness of your authenticity, of your wholeness. This is true relationship. It is found as you establish your connection with the Divine Oneness, re-claim your relationship with Light, and understand the need for expansion.

When you come into union with another being that has come into the ecstatic knowing-ness of their authenticity, then you are completing the expansionary process. You are joining Light with Light. You are expanding. You are bringing mutual understandings and experiences to each other, thereby offering back to God the expansion of Light through the experience. This has always been your mission here as a collective. Once this is achieved, you take it further.

When you and your partner bring that wholeness to another couple who have found their wholeness, you create a community of Light. You are all offering service to the Divine in the manner in which it is in service to the perfection. It is the reason you are Travelers[16] to begin with: to expand, to understand, to experience. Most importantly, bring all expansionary experience back to the Divine. This is a very simple and important concept; it is why you are here, and why you have always been.

During the Atlantean lifetime,[17] this concept began to unfold very beautifully. During this time, you had great understanding of the necessity of expansion and the importance of your mission as Travelers. It was also during this first experience of Atlantis[18] that your Divine communication was still uninterrupted and in direct contact with many Realms of existence.

Because of this understanding, and the direct communication with many other beings, there arose the first infiltration, or mutation of the energy. The ego came in and said, "Why do we need to give all this Light experience back? It is right here. We can create ourselves."

Once the ego became self-righteous, new beings were created by the Atlanteans. It is important to understand that this is what led to the end of the Atlantean time. It was the combination of the manipulation of DNA, the desire to become "god," and the desire to keep the energies within. The pervasive ego took hold and said, "We do not need Divine intervention. We live a long time. We have growth. We understand, and we do not need to give it back."

This was the ending of the cycle of gratitude, receiving, giving. This is the model of true relationship; it is a circle, and this is the key. All true relationship must integrate gratitude, receiving, and giving. This is the only way it can continue, and it must first begin with your own relationship with the Divine.

Remember that in the middle of the circle is wholeness. One must understand wholeness to stay in gratitude, receiving and giving. It is important to understand this model.

Each circle has the same rotating cycle.
The arrows represent: Gratitude, Receiving, and Giving.

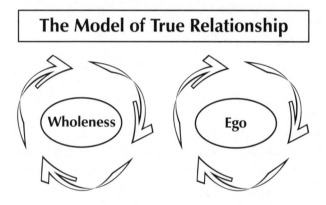

The Model of True Relationship

Wholeness

Ego

SRI RAM KAA: You mentioned that in the time of Atlantis, the knowingness of the couples and their giving back was unfolding as intended, but then there was intervention from others...

From yourselves. Let us explain. For many years, as you call them, during the time of Atlantis, all was proceeding joyously as part of the expansionary Light. The direct Light exchange with the Divine created the ability for ever more knowledge. Therefore, the more adept you all became. There was great comprehension about the many aspects and applications of DNA. This included DNA stranding and DNA coding. The greater your understanding of DNA and how to use it, the more you all became, shall we say, reluctant to do the mundane things necessary to support life. Tasks considered less important, such as harvesting and growing your own food, became the work of those considered to be "less than." It was a time of rapid increase in the energy of judgment and separation.

The concept of less than and greater than was a slow and steady perversion of energy that was introduced by invaders who interfered with your energy from afar. They were not present on Atlantis; they were simply available. They were Leumerians[19] who had fallen out at the time of Leumeria. During the first time,[20] they vowed to make sure that the experiment[21] would not continue, and are so far away from the Divine Light that they have forgotten that they, themselves, are part of the growth.

The perfection of their straying, combined with the perfection of their ability to no longer be connected, is most important. It offers great understanding as to where you are now at this time in your Earth history.

At the time in Atlantis of your greatest connectivity, and when civilization as a whole reached great levels of understanding, it then became easier to interfere with the energies. This statement may seem ironic, so we will explain more.

The energies of interference that were planted at this time were the energies of egoic outcome. Egoic outcome does not serve the model of gratitude, receiving, and giving. Egoic outcome only serves the I. "What's in it for me? What about me, and why me?"

It is the model you see before you now at this time in your collective experience as the expansion of Light. This model is once again present on this planet, and stronger than it has ever been. It has had eons of evolution, and like all energies, has had the time and ability to become ever more sophisticated. This self-preserving energy is indeed what has led to the mutation of the model, and why it is imperative to fully understand it.

Let us begin with an important premise: Egoic outcome only believes in gratitude if it serves the **me**. It only believes in receiving if it is for the benefit of the **me**. Know that it will only give if it believes it is for the benefit of the **me**. There is an easier way to say this. If it is not of wholeness, it is of ego, and that is the difference between the two models. One model has wholeness, one model has ego.

As the demand for those who could easily take over the mundane tasks increased, hybrids were developed to walk on the Atlantean surface. Part *animal, part of what you might call "human type," they were considered a triumph. They were of lower form, as you would describe them, easily manipulated, and very basic in their understanding and needs. For these beings, it was about food, sex, and existence, without any connectivity to Divine understanding. They worshipped that which was available to serve their needs exclusively, and saw their creators (the Atlanteans) as their gods. This was also the premise for many later misunderstandings that arose on your current planet during the Egyptian[22] dynasties; however, this is a discussion we will have later.*

Through this Atlantean manipulation of DNA, indeed by this great crime, for this is the only word we can offer, the ending of the Atlantean existence rapidly escalated. Through the engorgement of the ego, many had gone astray. There were those who were walking on the streets of Atlantis and working in the fields who had no understanding of the Light. They were incapable of understanding that they had been given DNA, yet had not been offered Divine connection, and the Elohim cried.

The Elohim crying; you ask how can this be? The Elohim cried out, knowing that which was created without the spark of Divine Light was also of love. Manipulated as it was, there was love available. Love is always available. The Elohim recognized it was important to offer and shower Light upon those who had been created in a lightless form. The only way to accomplish this was to ask all to take rest, to receive Light, and to begin again. This was how the decision was made to complete this second cycle of the expansion of Light.

SRI RAM KAA: I appreciate you sharing this. It seems to me that this must have happened over a great length of time.

As you understand time, yes.

SRI RAM KAA: So the ability to fashion another vessel or being from DNA then provided or stimulated further separation from the Divine principles?

Yes, and this is happening again now. Your planet is not too far away from coming close to doing this again. You are actually closer than your media would have you know.

Sri Ram Kaa: Yes. You shared with me at another time about the Merkabah Revolution,[23] which is just a continuum then of the separation consciousness?

Yes, this is correct.

Sri Ram Kaa: Is not also the Merkabah Revolution a yearning to reconnect?

ALL is a yearning to re-connect, even the creation of others. When beings are created, is it not taking the aspect of saying, "I yearn to connect so much that I shall create life myself?" This is why the Elohim cried, for even though it was a mis-understanding, or mis-direction of the love, the love indeed was there. Misguided by intent, it was the love for all that inspired the creation.

The Atlanteans had confidently declared, "We love our existence, we love this way of living; therefore, we shall create ever more to support it." For is it not true love that has inspired technology to where it is now? I wish to make this simple.

For example: "I wish to have my wife not work so hard, so I will create a washing machine." Is that not an expression of love?

Sri Ram Kaa: Love through an egoic filter.

Of course! This is the model that says I can be in gratitude, giving and receiving for as long as it serves me; this is the egoic model, not the wholeness model.

It is important to understand that when one removes judgment from the model being used; one sees that there is love, regardless of the model embraced.

This is the highest understanding of the Elohim. This is the non-interference pact, for would it not be easy for the Elohim to have interfered at any given time?

Sri Ram Kaa: How does the decision to rest come into alignment with noninterference?

The decision to rest offers continuation. After the time of Leumeria, after the time of Atlantis, there were periods of rest. These were not periods of ending. These were periods of rest, thereby allowing the expansion of Light to continue. Let us bring you to the now, for your question is what is happening, what are these energies, what is the now?

SRI RAM KAA: My question is, how may we all become ever more full with our choice to be here? I sense that these energies bring a great opportunity to all.

Yes, they do. We have offered these models to embrace with many more to come. It is the work of union, the work of beings of wholeness sharing their wholeness with other beings of wholeness. This creates a community of wholeness. Together you create an understanding of wholeness, so that the work of wholeness is expanded. People are seeking this energy, and it brings to all the alignment they seek.

You are at the time now where there is no time of rest that is forthcoming. It is the time of the great reunification. This is what has been waited for, and what was created at the beginning. At the time of the great reunification will come the time of the great movement forward. It is also the time of the great renunciation. There are many who will renounce many things.

SRI RAM KAA: Renounce God?

Of course.

SRI RAM KAA: Does this not spin into a whole other universe of dark expansion?

Everything expands; polarization is occurring. All will go home, and all will have their expected experience of going home. Soon there will be a great explosion of power on the planet. It will be small in magnitude in proportion to that which could be, or could have been. We cannot stop the explosion of power soon to be released. The aligned beings of Light, combined with our alignment energies, can help the impact to not be as dramatic. This explosion of power must be. It will escalate many channels of communication and openness, while also increasing polarization. Understand that polarization is needed; it is part of the balance.

The channels of communication are open. There are many energies that seek to interfere with humanity. There are many who seek to be in the service of your planet, and there are many energies seeking to be known.

67

*Simply stay surrendered to trust in the Divine supporting you, guiding
you. May each come to their temple as they are. Open your heart, be
available, know, see, do.*

*Many among you are servants, as many among you are pirates. That is
why you are in this experience of this density, to have all experiences. The
time of the slumber is over, yet there are those who sleep well.*

SRI RAM KAA: Yes. Truly a time of great choice.

*Yes, a time of magnificent choice and magnificent being-ness. A time to
understand all that will be, all that has gone before, and all that is now.
It is the time of the great reunification. Be fearless, be joyous! Joyous
morning. Joyous day. Namaste.*

*We are most graciously accepting of your love, and we offer you this
love in return.*

AWAKENING: UNVEILING AUTHENTICITY

Individuals awaken to their mission at different times. There are also
those whose mission it is to stay relatively asleep. Celebrate them! They
are doing their job. Many Light Workers and New Thought Practitioners
believe that everyone should see the world as they do. This enthusiasm
is not limited to any one belief system.

Souls that slumber and stay immersed in limiting beliefs are offering
you a tremendous gift. They provide you the discernment of your choice.
Without them, you would never know if you had arrived at your clarity!
Loving them unconditionally, as they are, is the ultimate test of your
truth. Or as Zadkiel once said: *"Sri Ram Kaa, some plants grow better in
shade. Love them all."*

Suspend your judgment, and practice noninterference. Trust that
ALL will find their way. The job for each and every one of us is to be
that which we are. Through our presence we will model and influence
others to become that which they are.

The return to loving global relationships seems awkward and inconceiv-
able at first. Truthfully, not everyone will immediately appreciate the gift
being offered. Authentic relationship begins with the Divine relationship

with Spirit, with your own Divine Self. Once you find the peace that is your truth, then you can be in healthy relationship with others. Without anchoring the Divine Self, outer relationships will fall short of true nourishment.

In the light of true love, healing happens. In the light of Divine surrender, individuals learn to trust their inner nature and thus find their divinity.

Searching for the fast track to personal growth? Here it is:

Love yourself unconditionally and trust your heart without reservation.

You don't need a technique or skill; you need only to trust your heart! Know that your heart will guide you to those who can teach you the skills you need to fully express yourself. If you want a deeper relationship with Spirit, you must ask for it! Connect with the Divine daily, and call in your guidance. Be willing to receive. Let go! Surrender what surrender looks like.

AWAKENING: THE EXTERNAL DOES CHANGE.

The process of awakening is readily mirrored in our external world. Spirit conspires to help you become conscious of what your soul is calling forth, usually by dismantling those things in your life which inhibit your true expression. Spirit will help you recognize what you truly need. Be open to how this expresses, as it may look like losing your job, a love partner or friend, moving to a new town, illness, even the death of a loved one. A seeming life crisis offers powerful gifts. Use these shifts to call forth a deeper understanding of your truth.

Reflect on the following question and allow yourself to really go deep with your response. What if tomorrow was your last day on the planet? Would your priorities shift? *Hmmmm?*

Yes, we are at the time of great change and realignments; therefore, it is time to get real. It is time to enjoy your life. True joy comes from alignment with your soul's path.

Use the external as a mirror to help you see what is shifting inside. There are no accidents. However, our interpretation of external events is often filled with human error! Let go of all interpretations and jump into the Galactic Flow that is upon you now.

Spiritual progress is not measured
by phenomena or altered states of
consciousness. Know that you are on the
path as you become the observer of the
moments of deep peace and trust. Unlock
the recognition that All Is Truly Well!
By recognizing the Divine Perfection in
everything, you will find Union in all its
manifest perfection.

~SRI RAM KAA

Chapter Seven

EXPERIENCING MULTIDIMENSIONALITY

The 2012 buzz has created a collective recognition that we are being actively encouraged to increase our awareness of multidimensional existence as being present now. The stimulus for this expansion in perception is available in many forms—literature, television, theatre, and of course, the Internet. Simply taking note of the recent deluge of extraterrestrially themed entertainment reveals a fascination with the unseen worlds, and often Hollywood seeds a fearful point of view into the consciousness of the mainstream. Yes, there is an imbalance being presented that offers a destructive and dark image regarding extraterrestrial life. Consider for a moment: If there is but one Divine Source, then extraterrestrials also come from that Source. So why assume that they are to be feared? There is an earthly bias that what is not initially understood should be not trusted. Recognize the gift in this, for even with its bias, it is simultaneously raising both terrestrial and galactic awareness for many.

How can this be? How can we be receiving messages designed to enhance the greater awareness of all, yet not be consciously aware of them?

Modern man seems to be trained from his earliest beginnings to be out-focused. Ironically, we are all born craving to ascend and without ever knowing what ascension is. As young children we crave to ascend through the steps of childhood, seeking to become "grown up," to be able to do grown-up things! We delight at our ability to ride a tricycle, and soon our consciousness is fixated upon mastering the two-wheeler! Whenever a level of mastery is attained, we immediately focus our attention on the next perceived level of achievement. It is as if our very cells carry a desire to expand to the next level of understanding, and are responding

What if we were able to fully recognize that this need, this yearning, is actually a stimulus to help us activate dormant memories of our true nature? **What if this propelling force that desires ascension is indeed a great gift to assist us in uncovering our Divine assets?** What if you could give yourself permission to accept this concept, right now?

You are the Expansion of Light.

~ARCHANGEL ZADKIEL

You are eternally shifting, moving and creating anew, over and over and over again. What a gift, the ability to continually expand. This is a process that cannot be terminated, for you cannot terminate expansion! It can only renew itself. Know that when you feel as if you are in a period when you are not expanding, that you are renewing!

Expansion cannot be terminated, because you are Light! Pure Light cannot be extinguished. You are the expansion of Light, the growth of Light, and the experience of the experience of the experience.

You cannot be extinguished or terminated. It cannot happen! Impossible! Only that which has density can be stopped.

SRI RAM KAA: Then only that which has density can have fear around it?

Correct! This is an important correlation for you to understand. Only in density does fear exist! There are, however, many different forms of density! Your mind immediately relates the concept of density to Earth, this Realm. There are other Realms that also have forms of density.

Fear exists in each of these Realms according to how the alignment of the molecules of energy are put together; simply said, the denser, the stiffer. Here on Earth, the fear is very stiff indeed. Remember that solid matter is simply Absolute Truth, covered by illusion!

Understand that through the fear, you know the truth of the density. There are many gifts for you to receive from fear; we will discuss just one gift now. As you see fear around you increase, and as fear becomes "stiffer," ever more rigid, ever more owning of itself, it is a gift to you. It is a vivid reminder of how dense this planet is, and how strong the illusion!

SRI RAM KAA: I'm reminded that until one stops the projection and experiences the bliss, it is hard to understand how deep the illusion is.[24]

Once you empower your Light, you effortlessly walk through all fear without fear. As you walk through fear, there will be those who say, "You cannot walk through that wall! The wall is made from ten feet of solid stone!"

The ten feet of stone, the thickness, has been created by the level of fear present, combined with the escalation of panic. It is built by a belief system in evil, fear, anger, jealousy, greed, and ulterior motives. These are all bricks in the wall. It has indeed grown thick and the mortar is very fast and hard, causing many to agree with the declaration, "You cannot walk through that wall!"

Know that Light (you) can walk through anything!

This is an important example. Fear is becoming the predominant experience on your planet now. You must recognize the gift of fear. It is reminding you that only in a Realm that has cemented itself in fear and bonded with the emotional belief in the reality of fear, can you find your truth again! It is simple to be Light once you understand that you are not fear!

Only the illusion you pretend to be can ever be part of the wall! You have choice! You can be part of the wall, or you can walk through it.

When you first begin, it is not uncommon to start walking through the wall, forget you are Light, and start believing in fear again. Yet, you are only five feet through and wind up becoming part of the wall. In essence, you are stuck.

You do not have to stay there! In that instant you can close the eyes of illusion, re-member, connect, call in, and continue walking. Your eyes of Light are closed to the world of illusion when you stand in the Truth of the Divine.

Remember, there is nothing to "see" in the experience of fear and density. People will say, "Oh yes, there is! There are trees and sun and grass and sky!"

This is absolutely true! Look at them through the eyes of Light. Understand them through the eyes of Light. Embrace your existence through the eyes of Light, not through the eyes of fear (illusion). This is when the Divine magnificence and the freedom that you seek connects to you. This can never be taken away!

Everything else is simply an illusion, an alignment of molecules that are fed very well! They are hungry, and are well fed. The collective belief system keeps giving them more food. Does it surprise you that they are so fat and healthy?

"Stay in the illusion!" they cry. "Stay here, and I will give you money. I will give you all the treats you want. Fancy clothing, ego gratification—I will give you everything that you want from this world of density."

YOU do not want it at all!

Yet, it is continually fed. It cries for food with demands. It is a demanding life-form of its own, not a universally evolved life-form. This life-form is tied to, and can only exist in density, so of course it seeks to preserve itself. It preserves itself by more food, more fear! Most importantly, it is limited in its expansion; it can only expand here.

So which life do you choose, which life do you serve?

It is OK to serve either the fear or the Light, for all paths are in perfection.

There are some who came here for the purpose of serving those of Light through density. They declared, "I want to serve the Light of the third-dimensional reality through deep-density fear. I will support the fear experience so that those who need to awaken their Light, can!" What a magnificent gift! Love them dearly.

There is great power when you are free from the illusion that disdains polarity. Recognizing the perfection of everything, including polarity, frees your consciousness, and it is your time to be free!

Recognize that the power within you is beyond the unlimited. The mind limits. You are on your path of mastership, and everything is unfolding. Release your frustration of time constraints. Many say, "I have heard it is unfolding and I do not understand why it is taking so long."

It is because you are fixated on the time[25] factor. When you release this factor and trust your guidance, ALL of the events around you become nourishing. You trust the gift of being Divinely protected, loved, surrounded, and sustained. Embrace and love ALL the events around you. Recognize the work of the Divine[26] through each one.

When you release judgment of right and wrong to become the observer of the events around you, time that is moving slowly will fold in upon itself, revealing that which you are waiting for!

Refrain from inactivity around this. So many misunderstand and say, "Oh good, I can hang out now."

You must claim and clarify your decision. "YES! I declare I am ready... I declare that I will, indeed, hold fast, and when I judge, when I see that which is less than my truth appear, I will be the observer. I will not be the jury!"

For as you are your judge, you also become your jury. This is even more dangerous, for then you sentence yourself to many things. Judgment is part of the illusion — mortar in the ten-foot-thick stone wall. This is often why you stop only five feet through; you judge yourself. "Who am I to walk through this wall? I am not ready. I have not studied enough, purged enough, read enough."

We assure you that you have all studied enough! You have all done enough!

Release the belief that YOU needed to do it all during this lifetime now.

Accept the truth that you are here because YOU have done it all!

Once you understand and accept this truth, what you seek to expand will harmoniously, effortlessly, and joyously float through you. It will appear and offer you all the comfort, security, and love you seek.

In this message Zadkiel refers to a "wall." This "wall" is the illusionary construct of Earth-based mass consciousness. Its bricks and mortar are comprised of belief systems, emotion, and the habit of being separated from our inner knowing. **How many walls have we all built in our consciousness as a result of our fears and doubts? How many barriers stand before acceptance, peace, and love?**

"Reality" here on Earth is a consensus model that allows for some limited diversity. At one time the Earth was known to be flat. At another time it was impossible for a human to run a mile in fewer than four minutes. These are just a few of the "realities" of the times in which these ideas were embraced by most as absolute truths. Yet each time these limited views expanded, there was a Quantum Leap in consciousness. After Columbus's famous voyage and other scientific revelations of that time, human consciousness took the leap that was later called the Renaissance. After Roger Bannister broke the four-minute mile in 1954, barriers to human performance began falling with regularity. We are again poised for another Quantum Leap. The Universe is conspiring to thin our veil of illusion and propel us into multidimensional understandings.

Fully opening to the concept of multidimensional existence and a multi-world reality can be seen as dramatic, and is even considered by some to be insane. Yet, there are two ways to contemplate the Divine beyond this world: Philosophically (head), or spiritually (heart). Philosophy without spirituality is simply mental speculation, and often leads to a closed loop of understanding.

Yet, spirituality without philosophy can become naïve superstition. We must join head and heart. Let your imagination burst through the walls of rational thinking and offer you the gift of connection to new possibilities.

Archangel Zadkiel frequently reminds us that the ashram is no longer a necessity for spiritual growth. We have within ourselves the Wisdom of the Universe. It is also important to remember that you have the ability to awaken from the illusion within any moment, literally right now. It is a choice.

LEARNING UNCONDITIONAL LOVE IN A CONDITIONAL WORLD

Tough playing fields produce strong warriors. Spiritual warriors who cultivate their heart and wisdom in spite of terrible odds and outside forces conspiring against them inspire our hearts. In the modern world we have, among others, Gandhi, Martin Luther King, and Mother Teresa as examples. The benevolence of Spirit knows that ultimately all will find their way home to the Divine. The Light within cannot be destroyed; however, it can often be disregarded.

To aid those who are awakening to their Divine Source, masters incarnate here from time to time to help us remember the way home. Great Light-bearers such as Abraham, Moses, Jesus the Christ, Mohammad, Babaji, Buddha, Lao Tzu, and many others have appeared on Earth to fan the flames of awakening. They left behind sacred symbols and a legacy of teachings. These masters remind us to seek a deeper understanding of Self than the veil has to offer.

Dogma was inevitable on a planet shrouded under veils of illusion. Belief patterns resulting in dogma began innocently as an effort to assist others in finding their way. The followers of the masters created dogmatic belief systems that became the accepted means of teaching the masters' works. It has been stated that it was not the intention of the Buddha to create Buddhists, and the same may be said for other great masters. The religions were created later. All dogma turns into a restrictive interpretation that becomes an externalization. Once a person accepts an externalized truth as "the way," that soul has disconnected from its inner Source, and will be entrenched in density, the playground of dogma.

Your ability to break free from this restrictive energy is contingent upon your direct mystical understanding. Without your direct connection, dependency upon an intermediary occurs. The pattern of disconnect or externalization will prevent you from finding the Bliss of Direct Communion.

Intermediaries, or wisdom holders, often support a system of hierarchy that generates a self-perpetuating system of separation. In many cases, religion has become a coping mechanism for the masses. It provides a sense of community and, for the most part, a direction, while quietly expecting that every member of the congregation will fall short of true Divine Expression. If you believe that you require help, then you are easily manipulated because you are judging yourself as deficient. If you believe that the answers lie outside yourself, then you will be held captive by those who claim to hold the mysteries in their secret chambers.

The modern mystic requires only one thing: Self-trust. The doors of knowledge have swung wide open! The secrets are revealed! For example: Tibetan Buddhism, once very reclusive and secretive, has swept across the planet, in part due to the constriction of Tibet by the Chinese. Other spiritual teachings as well are now available to all—the Truth cannot be available to only the few. Yet, out of habit, most people now look to a new authority for interpretation of Truth!

The guru has become a New Age author, charismatic minister, or a self-help authority. This transference may open you to some new information, but it will keep you ever one step removed from Source. Begin to trust yourself; it is at that point when you can claim your Divine Authority. You are a Master…You are the Guru!

The vibrational level of the planet offers energetic support for you to recognize Truth and reconnect with your soul's knowing. Until you open to your Divine channel within, the only empowerment you will experience from most external gurus is that of a spiritualized ego.

The ego will gladly pirate away your spiritual growth, for the ego seeks control. The ego is a pirate and a master of deception and disguise. For now, just understand that a true teacher is one who cultivates your freedom, not your dependency!

A true teacher will help you develop Self-trust, and nourish your inner knowing. A true teacher celebrates your growth, champions your freedom, and above all models this gift through their own life expression, not just through their words.

You know you are on the right path when you outgrow several teachers along the way! You will know you are on the right path when your inner life offers greater peace than anything in the outer world.

> You need not look for God
> Either here or there.
> He is not farther away than the
> Door to the heart:
> There he stands, waiting till
> He finds you ready to open the door
> And let him enter...
> There is only one thing you must do:
> Open and enter.

> ~Meister Eckhart,[27]
> Christian Mystic

Chapter Eight

ENTERING THE PYRAMID OF SPIRITUAL AWAKENING

As we navigate our third-dimensional[28] experience on this amazing planet we call Earth, there are four distinct strata of consciousness that offer us growth and recognition.

These four levels create the Pyramid of Spiritual Awakening *(see picture on page 82)*. As we explore this pyramid, it is imperative to recognize that any of us, at any time, can experience "the wall" that separates each stratum.

The Pyramid of Spiritual Awakening is built on the foundation of Density Consciousness. It is the level we agree to be born into and the one in which "the wall" first appears.

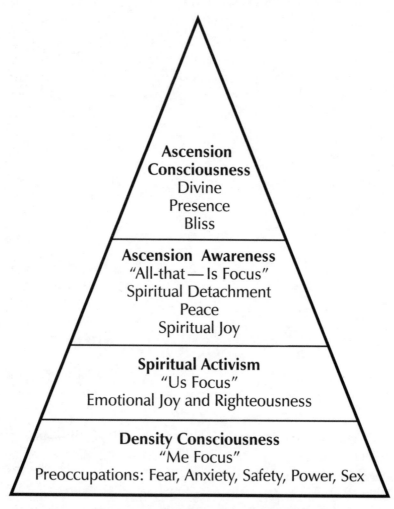

Pyramid of Spiritual Awakening

Density Consciousness begins as the stream of your reality that fears death of the body, believes in dualistic paradigms, *looks out for Number One*, and has a strong sense of right versus wrong. This stratum of consciousness also leans toward black-and-white thinking, identifies with group values and patriotic ideals, and enjoys the sense of belonging that comes through clubs and teams. Density Consciousness mistrusts strangers and respects all forms of socially acceptable authority, disregarding and downplaying inner authority. Refinements within Density Consciousness include higher orders of differentiation, such as a different team or game that seems more inclusive or evolved. However, characteristic of all players in Density Consciousness is an "us versus them" psychology with a strong sense of right and wrong.

However, even at its most sophisticated level, Density Consciousness exclusively trusts only externally validated truths, along with what it can see and touch. Density Consciousness also has a strong sense of who belongs, what is safe, and enjoys knowing the agenda for things. Spiritual Activism, on the other hand, is more flexible and tolerant.

The emotional experience of moving from Density Consciousness to Spiritual Activism at first feels empowering. Having broadened his or her playing field through activism, one begins to see a larger picture, and seeks to hold higher principles. Activism often inspires inner mandates of greater responsibility, bringing greater wisdom into the density. This seeking of greater unity is what moves the consciousness to embrace spiritual models.

Spiritual Activism offers a sense of purpose and greater meaning. Thus it is empowering by its very nature. It trains the ego to look beyond the me. This perspective shifts the focus to include the needs of others as being also important. In expanding identity beyond the me, activism expands consciousness itself. Activism takes a longer-term point of view, sacrificing near-term gratification for a broader reward down the road. Activism is mindful of the needs of others and is an evolutionary step forward from Density Consciousness.

Great social advancements, missionary outreach, and much of the human-development movement have been born from this stream of consciousness. It is activism, however, that when opposed, quickly regresses into righteousness, anger, and aggression, all of which are disconnects from Divine recognition and integration.

Density Consciousness and Spiritual Activism are both characterized by a sense of right and wrong, with Spiritual Activism offering a broader value system. Both strata are passionately committed to their agendas, and often bring great emotion to their battles.

While navigating our way through life, we create numerous events. And for every event, there are the emotional responses to them, especially as described in the first two strata of the pyramid. Together they create a loop that can easily ensnare us for years, or even a lifetime.

An event stimulates an inner response (emotion), and based upon that, we offer a behavior or action that generates a new response. The emotion fuels the cycle of the event-response loop. Like a wheel, it keeps generating and circulating thoughts, feelings, and behaviors. All of these are organized around the emotional body. By freeing ourselves to first recognize this, and then know the truth of our limitless existence (beyond emotional reactivity), we can release both the event and the response.

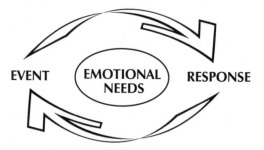

The Event-Response Loop

The event-response loop can create a whirlpool of attachment that draws one into dramatic entanglement with an inner dialogue or an outer event. The loop is fueled by emotion, and if the emotion behind your actions is fear or desire, then the energy generated by the loop will take control. These emotions tighten the loop into a limited number of acceptable cause-effect scenarios.

The response one offers to a trigger event is the result of their habitual orientation, emotional education, and level of consciousness. As long as an emotional need is in the center of the loop, a cause-effect cycle is perpetuated. Emotional needs, even needs for peace and stability, are based on the egoic perspective of the person. Thus, the event-response loop offers the ego a sense of identity, for it is in the movement or flow of emotions and actions that the ego is exercised.

Exercising the ego is a self-reinforcing confirmation, even if it hurts. The ego is more concerned with experiencing a sense of power, evidenced through exercising control over something, than it is concerned with pleasure or pain. Just as pleasure is generally reinforcing, pain also offers a sense of aliveness; thus, the ego easily becomes addicted to the pain.

The ego is like a child. It wants to feel important, and will therefore create and perpetuate pain and dysfunction to keep your attention. This attention empowers the ego and also the habit of pain. Is this truly the energy that you wish to reinforce?

Calling forth the energy of gratitude as your first response to an event brings spaciousness into the loop. This spaciousness allows for the possibility of cultivating a new perspective and loving responses. Gratitude is the choice of the conscious co-creator. The spaciousness of gratitude opens to peace and nonattachment, allowing for true acceptance and love to emerge. This consciousness offers an expanded event-response loop and is associated with the next strata of consciousness known as Ascension Awareness.

In Ascension Awareness, one begins to differentiate between soul-based joy and emotional joy. As one anchors their consciousness in Joy, personal emotional agendas do not surface. Ascension Awareness is an ascended perspective that sees the Divine acting in both sides of an argument. Ascension Awareness also embraces great trust in spirit, and thus patience and nonreactivity arise effortlessly.

As one embraces the energy of Divine Presence as a response to an event, there is no judgment, just Joyful Presence. The energy of the event-response loop expands even further into buoyant spaciousness. There is little or no "I agenda" to fuel the loop. This is the gateway to Ascension Consciousness. Some would call this Enlightenment—a word rarely used in our culture, as it is considered to be fairly out of reach. We experience and believe otherwise. Enlightenment is your birthright; it is what and who you are, and begins to be realized simply as the ability to love your less-than-enlightened aspects. The ego gradually dissolves in the presence of unconditional love.

The Ascended Consciousness knows that all sense of right and wrong is a human creation, a projection of personal agendas upon the density playground. With the creation of solid form comes differentiation and duality; it is simply part of the experience and no longer needed in the ascended strata, for its basis of necessity has ceased.

The event-response diagram offers a depiction of the shift in energy. It is your identification within the flow of energy that affects the loop. Having strong attachments tightens the loop. Residing in spacious consciousness allows energy to radiate more freely. The key to expanding peace and freedom in your life is to practice holding spaciousness.

The energy of gratitude and soul-based Joy are not contaminated by the emotional needs of the lower self (the ego). Wisdom, Love, and Divine connectivity become the natural influence of one's interactions. These qualities expand the playground and offer safety for all involved.

Ask yourself, "Are my responses to events feeding harmony or disharmony?" The answer is always simple from the spiritual perspective: **Anything that takes you away from pure Love and Joy is an investment in polarity.**

The energy on this planet is greatly aligned with Density Consciousness. This is what has brought us to this time in history. Density Consciousness gives birth to fear, polarity, materialism, mortality, and Earth-centric concepts. The expansion of Spiritual Activism has been rapidly growing since the 1960s and is attracting many at this time.

Undeniably, the energetic vibration on the planet has increased.[29] This increase stimulates and supports the rapid advancement in spiritual awakening. Spiritual Activism is the level of consciousness that accepts that there is a greater principle available (it does not matter which principle you subscribe to). From this level of understanding there emerges a seemingly universal code of right and wrong, and standards of behavior that are "good for you." While Spiritual Activism is more flexible and spacious than Density Consciousness, it simply brings the energies of Density Consciousness into an expanded playing field.

The United States has in recent years begun heated debate over the introduction of "intelligent design"[30] within its school systems. U.S. District Judge John E. Jones writes in his 139-page opinion: "We have concluded that it is not [science], and moreover that ID cannot uncouple itself from its creationist, and thus religious, antecedents." (CNN, 12/20/05, "Judge Blocks Intelligent Design.")

While the underlying motives for the intelligent design movement may be suspect, ID has surfaced as the perfect example of the "wall" that stands between Density Consciousness (science) and Spiritual Activism. Through this one issue, many are indeed breaking free of their traditional density alignments—only to find themselves aligned with a new, more sophisticated density concept (activism), that includes a spiritual context.

The 2004 U.S. presidential election was another wonderful opportunity to see the rise in Spiritual Activism. A faith-based presidential campaign rallied many aligned Christians to invest energy and money in the election. Were they voting for a man, or casting their ballots for principles that they believed should be universal? As we see the political campaign heating up for the 2008 election, has anything really changed?

Importantly, note that Spiritual Activism in this context also applies to New Thought or metaphysical principles. The broader view is applied. For this discussion, *spiritual activists* are defined as "any who embrace and act upon a belief system that differentiates between right and wrong, based on a sense of a higher (Divine), or universal order."

Regardless of the most persuasive arguments to support their highest expression, spiritual activists are all rooted in a belief in density. The world of experience has offered them an implicit fear of being taken over by a less enlightened system or group. Activism has an underlying "us vs. them" energy, even as it invites inclusion.

Spiritual Activism is actually the most challenging of all levels, as it has at its disposal the greatest ability to justify itself. It therefore masks the ego in universal principles. This is why it easily takes so many forms. Within Spiritual Activism there is no difference between the energy of fundamentalism, liberalism, terrorism, and other forces. Only the judgment of one set of values versus another claims the difference. Recognize that they are all vibrating at the same level within the context of the Pyramid of Spiritual Awakening, a powerful and sometimes disturbing recognition.

When Spiritual Activism no longer feels comfortable, one will immediately make a choice between two options. One will either head back into Density Consciousness, craving the simplicity of black or white choices (as in *The Matrix*'s pill choice), or one will springboard into Ascension Awareness. Either way, a choice is made and is a cause for celebration. Clarity is healthy regardless of the paradigm one chooses, for it aligns the soul's energy with a path of learning and action. When one makes a clear choice, the soul benefits from the wisdom offered by the consequences of the choice.

HOW DOES ONE BREAK FREE FROM SPIRITUAL ACTIVISM—OR DENSITY CONSCIOUSNESS, FOR THAT MATTER?

Both Density Consciousness and Spiritual Activism rely strongly upon belief systems. Beliefs are boundaries in consciousness, and all beliefs impede self-realization and true recognition of the Divine Source.

So how do we become free? Release judgment! Judgment aligns with Density Consciousness, and the release of judgment aligns with Ascension Awareness. This is a potent understanding, and it begins foremost with the recognition of the judgments within.

As we judge events and people, we generate separation from the Heart and Divine Flow. Judgment is a densification of thought energy, and does not easily allow for growth and transformation. Judgment objectifies the "other," or the object of the judgment. Judging yourself separates you from you.

Self-judgment establishes an inner polarity. Remember that all judgment wounds ... all. Once the pattern of judging is in place, it will apply universally to all things. Judgment will separate you from others, from yourself, and from Divine Flow.

Judgment expressed by those we consider our friends and loved ones usually triggers self-doubt. As you transverse density and make choices to grow, many who are unable to express their appreciation will instead express jealousy and fear through jokes or snide comments. Usually, they will direct their cynicism to the perceived cause of your growth (a book, a teacher, a personal-development course, etc.) rather than honestly share their fear or concern that you may be growing in ways they cannot understand.

Firmly ground yourself in your own opening, recognize their fear, and meet them there. Your friends' reactions are an amazing opportunity to be clear about your choices and not be swayed by their perceptions. Often, they are simply waiting to see if you are truly committed or simply off on a tangent. This is the power of a sincere choice.

We all seem to experience just enough pain and motivation to help us find our way. The universal intent is always pure; it is the distortion of the density world that makes growth a painful experience. We live in a Free Will Zone[31] wherein there is no interference from our Angels and Spirit Guides. They will only offer guidance and help to energize outcomes when asked. Spirit always supports our growth while simultaneously respecting our free will. Progression comes from your unrelenting yearning for Union. This yearning dissolves the grip of the ego.

Making conscious connection to your Angels and Guides opens your perceptual field and expands your ability to trust in the nonphysical realms. Remember, noninterference works universally—your Angels will not interfere with others. Universal balance will always be. Respect for all paths is a universal truth.

ARCHANGEL ZADKIEL: *We seek to bring you clarity so that you may gain a level of certainty that did not exist prior to this information. We do not seek to harm or cause confusion. We do, however, intend to assist you in shattering what is left of the illusion so that you may break free of all that binds you. It is time for you to know the Love of the Universe, the Love of the Union, the Love of Cosmic Oneness.*

There is much to say, and we search for the expression of words that make sense to you in this realm. This is a new quest for us, and for this one who is able to open her heart so big as to let us In-soul and speak [reference to Kira Raa].

We see the pain of the great divide, and feel the call to love. We hear the cries for completion. We are aware of all that you are searching for and seeking. For so long we have been present with you, hearing you, watching you, preparing you. While it may feel as if we have not been present, we have been with you since the beginning, loving you as a shelter of protection while you have had your chosen experience here.

We love you so much that we would not interfere with that which you chose. We appear to you now because it is the predetermined time. It is not that we have now chosen to simply appear; it is quite different than that. You agreed to this time for our appearance.

We know there are those of you who are most confused and feel as if this may be new information. Know that we are Messengers of Light who love you dearly, who love you so much as to have been supportive and nourishing of you on this entire journey.

It is most important that you do for others as we are doing for you. Be clear that this is the time of the choice of Love. There is great depth and clarity when we move from knowing about Love, growing into Love, and then breaking free to be able to choose Love with the full knowledge and clarity of what that choice truly is.

Divine Pure Radiant Love is the most powerful healing ray available to you while you are in density. It is the ray that is able to penetrate from the deepest Realms to re-activate your universal memory system. Yet it is the ray that you most often distort and cut off through illusionary belief patterns of what this is or should be. It is heavily conditioned. It is immediately begun for many in the shutting down process from birth. The mutation of what this pure ray, this purest Light is, begins with your first breath.

Our earthly veil is more than one of simple forgetfulness; it is a veil of separation and significant distortion. A soul, coming into a body, is predestined to forget its origin and mission. It must find its own way. For the Divine One inside of your body, this is where the fun begins. You get to play on the game-board of Earth and rediscover your greatness and mastery!

Over millennia, the veil has been manipulated by other energies to include significant distortions.[32] Belief patterns that are disconnected from spiritual truth, misunderstandings about the source of true power, fear of death, and many externalizations—all serve to pull your attention and energy away from your true spiritual purpose for being here.

The game-board of Earth has become a prison for the souls who are the Travelers—its level of difficulty has exponentially increased. Thus, once here, most souls find their intentions are distorted and that the cycle of reincarnation has become seemingly endless. Seeing through this thick veil is an extraordinary accomplishment, and now is the time.

REFLECTIONS

It is a uniquely Earth-based psyche that sees one point of view as being possibly better than another point of view. The Pyramid of Spiritual Awakening has a top and a bottom. At the bottom is the stratum of consciousness we have termed Density Consciousness. It is not located at the bottom because it is lower or less desirable than Ascension Consciousness. Rather, it is located at the bottom of the pyramid because Density Consciousness is foundational.

Density Consciousness is what you came to Earth to "do"! It is the quality of consciousness that is unique to this planet. Within Density Consciousness are levels of understanding or additional strata that could be discussed. However, this book's focus is to provide an overview of what is happening to consciousness in general, and to give you the practices and information that will help you gain greater clarity in your life. Through clarity, we make more aligned choices and can better direct our personal power toward the things that matter most to us.

We are not suggesting that everyone in Density Consciousness should move to Ascension Consciousness. It is important that each person serves the greater good from the level of participation that aligns with his or her heart at any given time. Your heart will guide you. Remember that some souls are here specifically to fully experience density!

No one is asleep here! Each is awake to their own personal level of consciousness. The activism aspect of our consciousness might want to judge some people's choices as crude, self-centered, or harmful. Rather than place those people on your favorite scale of judgment, consider instead that they are doing their best in any given moment. Consider that they are as awake as is possible at the moment, and that they too are on their soul's path.

Living in a society of great diversity in the expressions of conscious-ness means that you must make choices about your environment and circles of interaction. We do not suggest that you tolerate unkind actions of others or accept any form of abuse. We do suggest that you cultivate a sense of awe and detachment from the diversity of human understand-ings and behavior. We also suggest that "like attracts like," and that as you grow in unconditional acceptance toward our shared world you will attract ever more harmonious people and circumstances to you.

Perhaps you have read this chapter and felt challenged by the infor-mation. Perhaps you have made judgments about specific aspects of the material or the general content presented. Or maybe you have smiled at the material with recognition. Regardless of how this information has resonated with you, you now have the opportunity for greater recogni-tion of your conscious expansion, right here in front of you.

Many have asked us how we have been able to break free from the realms of Density Consciousness and Spiritual Activism. Consistently in the messages from the Archangelic Realm we receive the reminder to "keep your eyes on the Divine at all times."

As we navigate the Pyramid of Spiritual Awakening, we recognize that every choice we make carries us either toward conscious expansion or toward contraction and fear. By choosing to look for the Divine under-pinnings in every event and every interaction, we have surrendered our personal agenda for the Divine Agenda.

> *Hold the Truth of the Divine in your heart, hold*
> *wholeness in your heart, and there can only be*
> *one outcome, Divine Re-connection.*

> ~ARCHANGEL ZADKIEL

There are simple recognitions within ourselves that we have noted over the past several years of "living" this work. As we have witnessed our own evolution and that of many around us, the following universal steps have appeared as a way to navigate the Pyramid:

1. You must want to know the Divine. It must become an overwhelming preoccupation to fully know and re-connect with this energy. We found the four steps of Self-Ascension[33] most powerful in opening to the Divine.

2. This commitment is enhanced by being with those who can support your yearning. As you evolve in your own understanding, you may also find your social circle or geographic location shifting in ways you did not expect. New alignments naturally occur. Trust the movements and find those who are holding the Light.

3. Support yourself with environments that nourish higher vibrational experience. Pay attention to what you expose yourself to. Unplug from fear-based media and unhealthy food.[34] Evaluate your home environment. Let everything your eyes fall upon in your home bring you Joy. Release your attachment to the conventions of Density Consciousness.

4. Recognize and trust your own inner knowing. Listen more! Trust yourself evermore! Surrender the need to control your thoughts and simply be the loving observer of an amazing being … you.

5. Renew your commitment to conscious co-creation each morning. This will align your energy and ensure your progress. We found it simple to practice saying the words "Thank you" upon arising, and greeting each day with a smile of recognition.

PRACTICE

Take a moment and enjoy a deep cleansing breath. Let your body enjoy this one moment of deep connection. Allow yourself to experience a few more of these loving breaths. Now, ask yourself: "How do I feel about the information in this book so far? When I read this, what does my mind seek to tell me, and what reactions have I experienced?"

Gift yourself by taking this moment, even one minute, and putting down this book. Be present with yourself, your judgments, and your knowing. Do your best to simply be the observer without any response.

If you feel called, write down what you are feeling in this moment, and allow yourself to simply express without judging yourself. If you are reading this book with others, you may wish to simply dialogue about your experiences up to this point. Do your best to simply observe without judgment. This powerful gift of simple presence will open you to deeper recognition of your own "wall."

SURRENDER WHAT SURRENDER LOOKS LIKE.

Exploring the true meaning of this one simple sentence has offered us years of delight and joyful revelation. When we finally stop cutting deals with the Divine, the gifts that we receive are endless. This is one such gift. Imagine our delight when, at the end of a regular session with Archangel Zadkiel, the following prayer was delivered directly from the Lord of Hosts.[35]

Note from Kira Raa: The following prayer is one that Sri Ram Kaa reads often. My heart expands each time he does, as often his eyes are filled with tears of loving recognition. May your heart touch your Divine Awareness with the same connection to the love that you are.

GOD'S PRAYER

Allow me to lift you up from that which binds you.

Surrender unto me thy will, surrender into the Peace that
I AM, that YOU ARE, that ALL IS.

Surrender, and I shall be there. I AM always there.

Let me lift you up. Simply trust and fall into me.

Let me cradle you, and I will lift you up. I will lift you up.

Be of me, be as me, be with me.

It is right for thee to be with me. No fanfare, no illusion.
Just the deep peace of the knowing, and the deep
gratitude of the Being, I AM the One you seek.

I AM the One, the Presence, the beginning that has no end.

I have always been in union with thee, and thee with me.

Let me lift you up.

Allow me to fill you, allow me to be there for you, allow
me to be present in all things you do.

Surrender unto me and I will take thy hand and guide it.

I will guide thy fingers, guide thy hands, guide thy feet.

This is a blessing that has been placed upon you.

This is the Love of the Lord of Hosts.

There is no fear.

There is no judgment.

There is no reservation.

There is just Joy.

Walk through Peace. Walk through Love, and find the Joy
of the surrender into me.

Peace be with you as I AM Peace.

Chapter Nine

UNDERSTANDING
ASCENSION CONSCIOUSNESS

Having explored the realms of Density Consciousness and Spiritual Activism, let's continue traveling through the Pyramid of Spiritual Awakening *(see picture, page 82)*.

Ascension Awareness begins with the release of judgment of the self. The line between Spiritual Activism and Ascension Awareness is where most seekers find their midpoint in the wall. Expect little or no support from the density experience you are unplugging from. Many, if not most, of your best-intended family members and friends will tell you why you should not do it.

What if you could allow yourself to trust your inner knowing, even if everyone you considered normal said you were wrong?

Ascension Consciousness does not require a shaved head or funny clothing. It does require that you disconnect from the traditional event-response loop. At first that may seem radical to your friends and even to your own ego.

Heart: The Harmonic Pulse of the Universe

~Archangel Zadkiel

Recognize that in the heart center, in the space of being fully aligned with the harmonic pulse of the universe, one has put the I's to rest. The I's are no longer the preoccupation, and have found their way into choice.

One can only hear the harmony of the universe from the heart. Within the heart, one hears the soul sounds of Truth. When the I's become dominant and take over, the heart cannot be seen or recognized, especially when the I's are determined through the eyes of density.

The greater question is always, "Do I choose the path of the heart, or do I choose the path of the I's?" This is a simple and nonthreatening way to make the choice, rather than by asking, "Do I want peace, or do I want chaos?"

Dearest children, you must know that the Earth you seek, the Nirvana you create, the pleasure, the Joy, the unity, is already here.

It is not something you need to be searching for. It is already here! All you must do is keep your eyes on it and train yourself to move into it.

Breaking free from Spiritual Activism is indeed far more complex than releasing Density Consciousness. This is due to the broad acceptance of Spiritual Activism. Ironically, it is this approval that creates the wall! Spiritual Activism is simply an egoic refinement.

There is another simple way to break free from Spiritual Activism: Recognize and embrace the love within yourself. This is far beyond the romanticized idea of love that is commonly accepted on our planet. It is the simple recognition of your Universal Connection with all. Being unconditional in self-love is the same as unconditional love toward all. As you forgive yourself, you forgive others. As you accept yourself without judgment, you stop judging others.

Discernment is the quality of detached observation, free from emotional needs.

Judgment is discernment with an attitude. You do not need to agree with all expressions of light; you simply need to release the judgment of them. The gift of Ascension Awareness is recognizing that you have evolved. You are now creating on a bigger canvas, one that is beyond judgment, and is rooted in Divine Love. Yes, this takes practice. As you practice the release of judgment, you must accept surrender as well. This will return you to trust and love. It will propel you into Ascension Consciousness.

Divine Love is the practice of reconnection to your Ascended Heart.

The year 2012 is rapidly approaching, and with it comes the opportunity for a Quantum Leap in consciousness. Everything that you have experienced in every lifetime has culminated in your presence on the planet now! You have chosen to be here at this momentous occasion.

- 2012 is not Judgment Day.
- 2012 is not the end of the world.
- 2012 will not magically transform us into a Golden Age.

Yet, if enough people gather their consciousness around any one of these beliefs, the state of affairs will indeed gravitate in that direction. You are *that* powerful! Your creative power has never been greater than at this time in history. This is why we encourage you to awaken to your true energy. A conscious co-creator has a lot more to offer back to the world than does a slumbering powerhouse!

Embracing the "top" of the Pyramid, or Ascension Consciousness, is not a level to attain—it is a presence of being that embraces all aspects of your expression as Divine Love. It is a state of blissful flow that offers great Light and service to those in other states of consciousness. To do this, you must understand the difference between connectivity and attachments, or you will not be able to anchor in the bliss.

Ascension Awareness is the state of consciousness in which issues of density no longer grip you; however, you still have an investment in the third-dimensional world. Ascension Awareness offers a bridge to higher dimensions, translating worldly power to spiritual empowerment. It is an anchoring in Peace, Love, and Joy, rather than in attachment to drama, power struggles, and ego needs.

The Pyramid reminds us that our evolution as conscious beings requires a transition through each state of consciousness. Be grateful for them all. Each level of experience refines your discernment and further opens your heart.

The Difference Between Connectivity and Attachments

~ARCHANGEL ZADKIEL

Soon a grander scale will appear before you, and in the transition, chaos is irrelevant. Why do you give credence to the chaos during the time of chaos, and believe the chaos is real, necessary, tragic, awful? Know the perfection of the chaos as it calls together hearts of wholeness and Oneness. Remember that chaos is an illusion.

*Remove the obstacles presented from your consciousness and honor them as gifts. Be present with that which is present within you. **The Joy of Oneness, limitless expansion, wholeness, and integration—this is the truth within.***

All illusion is dropping. Even the fear will find less resistance, for it is time to let it go, on all levels. Know this: There is only one challenge, the challenge of connectiveness. When anything is not flowing, look at the challenge presented and ask, "Am I connected? If I am connected, what is it I am connected to?"

This is a good question. It is simple to have attachments; it is simple to attract clinging attachments. This is not connectiveness, and it is an important distinction to understand. There is only one true connective-ness that offers you complete nourishment, complete energetic feeding, complete flow. It is connectiveness with the understanding of the limitless, boundless Joy of the Divine. This is true connectivity.

Yet, in the truth of this, many hold on to their connections. They claim connection to material things, persons, events, or beliefs. What must be

clearly recognized is that they are not connected at all—they are attached!
Know that all attachments can be removed.

Connectiveness is spacious. When one is connected, one has the
expansiveness necessary to experience expansion. One is in the Divine
relationship of connectivity. This relationship offers giving and receiving
simultaneously. It is without judgment, without fear, and in complete
trust and love. This is very different from attachment, and shows a vital
distinction—the difference between connectiveness and attachment.

Attachment can be simply cut away. Attachment is a manipulator as
it is manipulated. Attachment has rules, and attachment has caveats.
Attachments have all of the necessary strings that hold us captive in
our thoughts, captive in our patterns, captive in our habits, and captive
without the freedom of connectivity.

You might ask, "How do I know? How do I know the difference
between connectivity and attachment, and how can I possibly understand that difference?"

Connectivity creates a spaciousness of energy that is physically comfortable. It completely encompasses you as a pure crystalline bubble. It
nourishes you. Connectivity offers the spaciousness of a peaceful mind,
an open heart, and giving hands. It has no judgment, and it fills you. You
are nourished by the Love of God or the universe.

Attachments…you feel them in chakras,[34] and you feel them in the
emotional body especially. Many have extensive attachments in their
sixth and seventh chakras, many more than they are aware of, because
they are so comfortable being attached. When one has these attachments
in the sixth and seventh chakras, they are also blind to them. This is the
intent of the attachment; it is meant to hold you in a specific space. That
is another difference between connectivity and attachment.

You can be held or you can be free.

WHAT ABOUT FEAR?

Fear results when you separate from Source. Fear is a dense and powerful
energy that we have woven into our basic orientation toward life. We
fear death, change, wild animals, strangers, aliens, foreigners, growing

old, getting hurt, feeling sick, losing our money, losing our beauty, losing our lover… Fear is everywhere.

False understandings are always the basis of fear—always. The antidote to fear is connection to Source, aligning with your authentic energy, your soul. No amount of skill development or training will eliminate fear from your life. Only true Divine alignment uproots the trembling shoots of fear.

Galactic energy that is flowing onto our planet is contributing to the energetic upliftment of all inhabitants of Earth. This energy is accelerating our sense of time and stimulating greater polarity on the planet. The energy fuels all levels of consciousness. That means fear is accelerating as well.

Fear is a potent and fertile energy that rapidly supports and seeds further contamination of consciousness. We define "contamination" as anything that is unlike love. If one is in fear and holding an expectation about the behavior of others who subsequently fail to meet that expectation, the result is anger.

For example, suddenly losing your job will trigger anger if you were holding a conscious or unconscious expectation of job security. Similarly, if you receive a life-threatening diagnosis from your doctor, you may feel fear and anger, just like the person who suddenly lost their job.

The fear-anger loop is a typical event-response that is perpetuated throughout society. Fear is the inner experience, and coupled with a judgment will likely result in the experience of anger. Anger is an action emotion, usually out-focused. Thus, once anger is felt, your ego will likely impel you to take some form of action. Typically, that action is motivated by a desire for reassurance that you are safe or acceptable. Anger seeks to bring control back to the individual who experienced sudden fear. If your motivation is to feel emotional joy, then the fear-anger cycle will continue. This is because emotional joy is an ego need, and as such it is dependent on externals. That is, your emotional joy is dependent upon a condition. Your emotional peace depends upon a job, good health, a lottery win, a new lover, etc. Thus, the fear-anger loop will always be lurking just below the surface of consciousness, waiting for the next event trigger to react to.

Following global events never fails to demonstrate the fear-anger loop in action, especially in political confrontations. When the fear and the anger are not quickly dispelled, then hatred emerges.

It is a simple formula: **FEAR + ANGER = HATRED**

It doesn't take much fear or anger to produce hatred; it just requires that both energies be present. Within group situations, not every member of the group has to hold both emotions. Some could be in fear, some could be angry, and others could lash out in hatred.

Hatred cannot be resolved through negotiation. You cannot resolve hatred through contracts, guarantees, or military balance. Unless the parties are able to walk into their fear and resolve the fear, peace is not viable.

Fear is the foundation of the discontent. On a personal level, fear must be faced. You must make friends with your own shadow and integrate the experience of fear into the wholeness of you. Integrating the shadow is a homecoming of sorts, for it opens you to disowned energies. To face your fears by stepping into them means they will be resolved permanently! This is how you find wholeness.

We cannot expect countries to behave any differently than is dictated by the consciousness of their citizens. Fear is a habit. Fear and anger are tools used by those who wish to control the masses to influence outcomes. Political conditions around our globe offer many examples.

HOW DO WE RESOLVE THE FEAR-ANGER LOOP?

Gratitude will immediately disarm the egoic drama. By choosing to be grateful for an event that stimulated anger, you are empowering yourself to recognize the gift before you. The event served to bring unconscious fear to your attention. The event made you aware of an automatic anger response. The event therefore has given you a wondrous "wake-up call."

Can you accept the gift? It is in that moment that you can embrace yourself as a Conscious being who is thankful for the experience. You are gifting yourself by accepting that you were unaware of your attachment to fear-based belief patterns. Through attentive gratitude, your energy will immediately expand, and you will see how insidiously limited and limiting your ego is. Through gratitude, your ego will learn that it is safe to show up without damning or being damned, and through gratitude you will expand beyond the ego's responses. You will generate an energy of trust and love for all those around you, and through that emanation you will cause those people to become more aware of their automatic event-response loops.

Awareness without judgment heals. That is the quality we call Presence, an awareness grounded in love.

True Freedom

~ARCHANGEL ZADKIEL

True freedom comes from connectivity to the Oneness at all times, or what you call bliss.

SRI RAM KAA: How can one function in the density without belief patterns?

By knowing and shifting to the deep awareness of connectivity. This is accomplished when you hold gratitude for every event, every experience. Deep connectivity offers recognition through the field of density that you function in.

When you go into your heart center, you recognize connectivity and Oneness. From there, everything becomes illuminated. Everything is known as One. Connectivity and authenticity are both the same, are they not?

When one is living in the connected state, authenticity is all there is. **Authenticity cannot live or survive in the realm of attachment.**

There has been much discussion about attachment on this planet and what it means. What are you attached to? We are discussing energetic attachment. When one releases energetic attachments, one exists in the realm of complete connectivity. Everything else falls into place. Once here, you do not need a set of rules to live by. All self-expression becomes the conscious and expansionary presence of bliss.

LIVING IN BLISS

Living in bliss, one does not need to be reminded of the rules. Ascension Consciousness is living in the Joy of Divine Connectivity. From this spaciousness one understands completely, and the questions disappear. Embracing gratitude for the perfection of all paths, knowingness, and love, combined with the true surrender and release of all judgment, the fullness of life is experienced.

Only when one is living in the world of attachment energy does the need for rules arise. You are told, "Do not do this. Do not do that. You should do this; you should do that."

This is because attachment energy separates you from yourself! Your true consciousness and ability to see is interrupted by the pattern of attachment energy. When one is attached to an outcome, then all decisions, movements, and energies are directed toward the outcome. Attachment energy thereby circumvents even the purest intent.

You can see how this becomes very challenging, especially in the case of a pure intent. If your outcome is to serve love, for example, then how can it be an attachment? Simply remember, any attachment, whether perceived as positive or negative is still that, attachment.

HOW TO RELEASE ATTACHMENT
AND EMBRACE CONNECTIVENESS

Be Love. Be Service. This is how you surrender the outcome. Be that which you seek. Be peace. This is true connectivity. When you are that which you seek, you no longer need to be concerned about the outcome.

Some will say, "Oh, I am still very attached to having a big house. I am very attached to having lots of money, success, and worldly acclaim."

These manifestations do not exist in the Divine Realm; they are material attachments. When one is tied to material attachments, it is simply impossible for one to be in their connectivity. This is the pattern that interrupts consciousness.

*We are not suggesting that one must surrender everything to move into connectivity. We simply ask that one shift their consciousness to **being*** *peace, being Love, being Joy. Let everything else be a product of that. All of your material manifestations will then reflect this inner harmony, and abundantly support you. The attachments will be powerless.*

The time on the planet is here when all are able to walk in connectivity—it is not exclusive or elusive! It does not take years of practice and study. It is for anyone who desires to go into their heart and be that which they seek. Claim it now. Know it is yours.

It is that simple.

What Archangel Zadkiel offers to us through this discernment is the ancient Hindu recognition of *Advaita*, wherein one fully realizes their existence as non-dual: anchored in Ascension Consciousness, embracing multidimensional existence, and knowing the bliss of Oneness.

In a world that wishes you to be attached to fear, and to crave safety, is it not a gift to abide in Advaita?

Finding your way through Density Consciousness is a challenge at best. The veil will enfold and unfold an infinite variety of forms and possibilities before you, for the veil is supported by the projection of human consciousness upon it. It is a wondrously intelligent, self-perpetuating creation, that will seek to keep the cocoon of density snugly wrapped around all who allow it. That is its purpose, and it functions well. It is not "out to get you." It exists to help you find your mastery.

This is why Archangel Zadkiel constantly reminds us to hold the energy of Joy. Remember that true Joy is an emanation from your soul; it radiates through the cocoon. The vibration of Joy will lift your energy so that you might find the way. It is from the energy of Joy that you will find the true Torchbearers, those who are radiating the Light of Divine Connectivity. These beings will help you ignite your light.

This is why dogma, by its own design, is unable to offer liberation; it only offers education. Divine Connectivity is an energy alignment. You can use the energy of these turbulent times to rise above duality.

The Buddha is credited with having said that once people hear of Nirvana, they will ultimately seek and find it. So it is with Ascension Consciousness. We believe that all souls hear an inherent call to Oneness. Many do not realize that in their choice of behavior they are actually following the call to Oneness.

Each will find their way back to Source. When they reunite, they offer the gift of their travels to the Oneness. This is why noninterference is the expression of one who resides in true connectivity. To interfere with the path of another would limit the richness they can offer to Source upon reunion. To interfere with another is to disregard and disrespect the Divine Intelligence.

ALL SIX BILLION PATHS ARE PERFECT!

Ascension Consciousness is not a singular path; it is a doorway. This opening is a gateway through the third dimension. People who have "died," or who have left their bodies, have the opportunity to reside in Ascension Consciousness, and many carry their attachments with them from incarnation to incarnation.

IT IS NOT NECESSARY TO DIE IN ORDER TO RESURRECT!

Ascension Consciousness is a choice that you can make now. The energies of these times make this possible for all who wish to choose it. Of course, that choice is yours! Making the choice involves coming to the recognition that you have done this all before. Sure, the details may have changed, but the recognition that you are a soul in a body, awakening into full expression, must be cultivated.

The gift of the path leading to Ascension Consciousness is the opportunity it affords you to consciously co-create. You also experience the bliss of Divine Union while still having a body.

There are ramifications from this choice as well. Strong attachments to the creations of the world of density will impede the lift into Ascension Consciousness. That is, your attachments will keep you engaged in the third dimension. For many, this may be attractive. For others, it's more of a "been here, done that" kind of experience…they are ready to move on.

Regardless of whether you think you are ready, the Path of Self-Ascension will reveal where your attachments lie. Each time they show up, you're invited to choose again! The process is one of walking forward and knowing your destination is assured, as long as you return your sight to the Divine with regularity.

ASCENSION DOES NOT HAPPEN TO YOU; IT WILL HAPPEN THROUGH YOU!

Practice

Take a piece of paper and write down how you would create your world in 2012. What is it you seek? What is the energy you wish to call in for yourself? If all your financial and emotional debts were paid, then what?

After you create the list, go back and review it. As you do, carefully determine which items demonstrate attachment and which embrace connectiveness.

What if everything you seek is given to you...then what?

Take your time with this practice. You may even wish to repeat it. Most importantly, gift yourself with being completely honest about what you see.

Chapter Ten

HELP ME TO UNDERSTAND THE FIFTH DIMENSION

Knowing that we are approaching a great shift, and that the paradigms of yesterday are disappearing faster than new ones can be created, where is this bringing us?

We have already established that the nature of the soul is to be active. We are ever-expanding beings of Light Consciousness who are collectively expanding through density to reunification.

Each expression of life has the opportunity to choose how this expansion will manifest! We have indeed expanded density as far as it can go. To take density any farther would be to simply recycle it, a redundancy that would offer nothing new to Source. Thus, the next step for light's

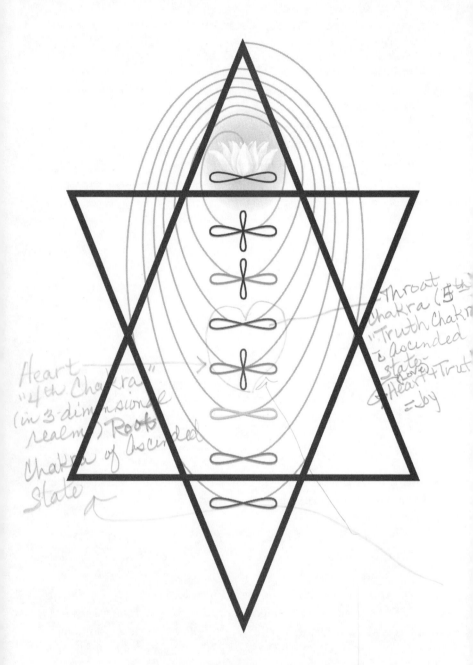

Self-Ascended Chakra Portrait

expansion is to expand through the density and reunify the individual streams of light into an expanded whole.

ARCHANGEL ZADKIEL: *"Why are we here? What is my mission? What is my path? What do I do? Is this the right career? Is this the right boyfriend, girlfriend, whatever?" These are the questions that we hear from you often. We are here to share with you that it is the time of perfection. It is the time of the unification of the One within.*

It is your time of living in the Ascended State, and recognizing that you are in the fifth dimension now. Only you must choose to be there, and understand what this is. It is not a state of being that is coming. It is not a state of being for which you must learn more, do more, be more. All you need to understand is that this Earth is the hologram, and it's a fun one, is it not?

It was October 30, 2004, when Archangel Zadkiel joyously announced to us all that the choice of how we were to continue living on this planet was imminently before us. The hologram of this Earth was rapidly polarizing, and we were at the time of ever greater choice. Zadkiel's announcement generated many questions and realizations.

One of the most important recognitions from the Archangelic Realm is the understanding of the Self-Ascended Chakra Portrait (*see picture*).

This offers a depiction of the human chakra system when the chakra energies are at peace. Instead of experiencing each energy center as a swirling whirlpool of energy, the chakras of Ascended Beings are in a state of Divine Balance, as indicated by the infinity symbols. With Zadkiel's announcement of the fifth dimension being available now, the chakra portrait made ever more sense.

As we embrace the state of Divine Union, our chakras flow as balanced, infinite spirals. The state of nonattachment allows energy to rise and center in the heart, offering connection with true Peace, Love, and Joy.[36] The Ascended Heart is represented by two intertwined spirals. This chakra is the first to have the double-spiral energy.

The heart expands into multiple expressions of energy as we open the higher gateways to multidimensional expression, and therefore align with Divine Love. This conscious alignment serves as the potent reminder that only love is real!

ARCHANGEL ZADKIEL: *The red, the yellow, and the orange,[37] dearest chil-*
dren, are chakras of the third-dimensional realm. For many years you were
taught to send energy down into the planet for releasing and clearing.

Dearest children, it is the time of the release. It is not the time of holding
tight. These red, orange, and yellow chakras are calling to you. They are
saying, stay here, pay attention to me. They want you to be worried about
safety, and to embrace fear. These chakras call you to have many issues with
clarity, and none of these are real. The only issue ever needing attention
is the one that takes you away from the truth of your Joy.

Remember the truth of who you are by saying "thank you" to that which
takes you away from the moment. See it as a circle, in complete perfection.
The circle begins with the chakra calling you, continues with the energy
desired, and completes with your gratitude for the recognition.

As you begin releasing the bondage of these lower three chakras, know
that they will always be present, because you are still here. These chakras are
necessary to sustain your body. Know that this is their primary and highest
function, to provide you with the opportunity to walk, to embrace, to enjoy.

ACTIVATING THE ROOT CHAKRA OF THE ASCENDED STATE

Take your right hand and place it over your heart. This is the root chakra[38] of
the Ascended State. This is the truth of who you are. This is the root center.
It is not the root of the third-dimensional experience. When you need to
make any decision, at any time, on any issue or opportunity, start here,
and then take your energy up.

The root of the Ascended State of Consciousness is the heart chakra. The
truth of who you are is the second chakra of the Ascended State.[39] When
the heart chakra and the Truth chakra are united, only Joy can come from
you. Only Joy can be you.

When the ego claims to not know how to feel about this new information,
know that it is an expression of the lower three chakras! You may think it is
your mind speaking, when it is the lower chakras controlling the mind.

Your mind is a beautiful gift, and it is your servant. If you are living
and carrying the root energy of the heart in to all that you do, then you are

*able to effortlessly release the mind back to its true service. The mind must be your servant. You are **not** the servant of the mind. Anytime you find yourself being a servant of the mind, simply ask which one of the chakras — red, orange, or yellow — has a grip on you. It is one of them, always.*

Simply take your hand to your heart. Allow yourself to release the fear, release the anger, and release all that has trapped you in the density of the third dimension. This is what keeps you from seeing and expanding into the Truth. The heart and the Truth together bring only Joy. This is all it can bring. Remember, if it does not bring you Joy, then why are you doing it?+

With the heart and the Truth together,[40] it is natural to have the vision of the universe in front of you. It is our gift to the world that we teach you, the teachers, how to bring others to life in the true center of the Ascended State. Give yourself the gift of living from the heart. It is the way you begin.

Learn to lift into your true Divinity without any fear. Know that you are Divinely supported, protected, and loved beyond measure. It is time to open your true vision, and receive.

POLARITY—THE PLAYGROUND OF EXPANSION

*Understand that this world is the playground of the expansion. Within the playground of the expansion there are many expressions. Many! As you are light expanding, as you are bringing this gift of wholeness to the whole, there is a great re-unification of Oneness. A time of great Joy! Yet with the time of Joy upon you, the question arises: **"Why is there so much polarity,** and why is it growing?"*

We come to share with you, dear ones, that this must happen. This is part of the expansion. Love it! Embrace it! Through this joyful embrace, you will understand the gift you are being given.

Know that within polarity, you are able to find the gift of light, and in the gift of light, you are expansion. In the expansion, you are able to claim your own wholeness. You came here to experience this ability. To live in this hologram!

LEARNING TO DIMENSION SHIFT

Let us now discuss the fifth dimension, for it is time for you to practice dimension shifting. As you practice stepping in and stepping out, it is like stepping into a tub of warm water. When you first get into the tub it is the perfect temperature, yes? You make it all nice, you put in what you like, you step in and enjoy.

This is what the third dimension is about—it is a big tub! Everyone puts in whatever they want and this is good. It feels good. You test the water and slip into the tub fully comfortable. However, if you stay in it too long it gets cold, or uncomfortable. It is at this point that you realize it is time to get out of the tub.

Sometimes you stay in too long or you try to add more hot water. This is very funny. "I will add more. I will try to make it hot again." But it is never quite the same, is it? No! This is very much like the third dimension. It is the tub of illusion.

You don't need to add any more hot water; it is time to get out. Yes! It's just that simple. When you know it's time to get out of the tub, that recognition feels good too, does it not? You can put on a warm robe, slippers, whatever feels good, and you are comfy again, and in a new state of being. Refreshed, relaxed, having had the bath!

You see, you are getting out of the bath and it is time for the new robe. The comfy slippers are indeed waiting. They have always been there. You simply need to slip them on, and say "Yes!"

As you give yourself the gift of moving into the Truth of your Ascended Heart, there is only one thing you need to do: remain focused on the Truth of the Divinity that you are, at all times.

Sometimes you may say, "I don't know how to do this! There is so much happening. How can I stay in my Divinity? I do not know how to do this! I got a bill today. I got a letter today." Sometimes you just wonder how to stay focused on this thing called Divinity.

Your strong mind comes forward with many precepts about Divine Focus. You assume that you can only do this during meditation, or when in a room with others of like mind. Then, you come forward with the perceived "real world," and the declarations: "But you don't know where I work! You cannot stay in Divinity where I work. It's impossible!" Or, "You don't know my partner!" You don't know this; you don't know that.

So we offer you the key to unlocking this mystery:

Stay focused on the Joy that you are. In your Ascended Heart is the Truth of the Joy that you are. In that Joy is the perfection of every moment, within the moment, within the moment. Here is the dimension you seek. Here is the truth of your being. **You are a spark of Divine magnificence.**

What Archangel Zadkiel so clearly points out for us in this revelation is that our true purpose and service is to simply return to the loving truth of our Being. When we embrace this Truth without reservation, then our very presence offers all those around us the same opportunity. Regardless of your occupation or living conditions, if you see the Joy simply in being, then you are truly of service. This is a powerful discernment. Within this Truth is freedom from the chaos of the third dimension.

A powerful door opens when we realize that everything we do is in service to the Divine. We must simply desire it to be from an open and sincere heart. Often, at the monthly discourses, Archangel Zadkiel asks for questions from those who are in attendance. The following is one such question.

QUESTION: Are there certain colors[41] for the new chakras, and especially for the new root chakra?

ARCHANGEL ZADKIEL: *Such a good question! We will describe the color of the Ascended Heart today for you. The Ascended Chakras are all interwoven bands. As you move ever more into the Ascended State, and start living in the root chakra of the heart, the chakra no longer spins as an orb.*

As you go into the heart chakra and make it the root chakra of the Ascended State, the chakra becomes the sign of unification [above]. In this

state of Oneness it looks like what you would call the symbol of infinity. The color is crystalline emerald.

There is, however, another infinity symbol that intersects this one at the Ascended Heart. It is the golden spiral, which meets with this emerald spiral, and the heart becomes the double spiral. It is the true root, with the crystalline emerald and the golden. It is most amazing! It is the new strand of the Ascended State. Know this!

You ask, "How do I ascend? When do I ascend?" We hear all these questions and find them so funny! It is hysterical to us, because how can you ascend to that which you have always been? This is who you are. You are simply calling in recognition as you release the veil of the third-dimensional hologram.

It is time for you to understand the truth of the crystalline beings that you are, the truth of the light that you are, and the wholeness that you carry. The rainbow that you are creating and calling back to wholeness is beyond the visualization of what you call an eye. We will offer you words and descriptions that will help your re-membrance.

Embracing the state of your Ascended Chakras is usually accompanied by physical shifts or changes. Yes, your body is shifting with these energy movements, and as with any form of exercise, when you have not used a muscle in a while, it may at first resist the workout.

Having experienced all of these energy shifts, the Archangelic Realm offers great clarity and a synopsis of what you may expect. Once you are aware of the "symptoms" of Ascension Energy integration, it becomes simpler to accept the flow of energy without resistance, and the physical responses gently dissipate into loving acceptance.

Time is folding in upon itself! As the energies on the planet rapidly escalate, your **third-dimensional experience IS SHIFTING!**

The Ascension Energy is calling you! With the entrance of the energy of the fifth dimension, many of you are experiencing changes in your body, mind, and emotions. The 3D "experts" would call these experiences "symptoms"! In fact, they are Ascension Acceleration Energy Experiences!

This list has been compiled at the request of the Archangelic Realm to offer you reassurance as you walk through this process of rapid integration.

Know that these energies appear as "markers along the way." They are signs of your expansion!

If you are experiencing one or all of these energies, we encourage you to:

Breathe, Laugh, Smile, and KNOW!

AAEE CHECKLIST

1. Headaches: May be experienced as nonlocalized pressure in the head, or as waves of pressure that seem to move. Third-eye, located between the eyebrows, pressure.
2. Visions and/or new "sight." Your vision may seem to be shifting, or be unstable. You may feel you require glasses one day, then shift into much sharper acuity the next day. You may be certain you are "seeing" someone/thing out of the corner of your eyes. A deepening sense of the ability to "see."
3. Sleep pattern interruptions: This takes on several different forms. The most important thing is to allow the energy to flow. Try not to resist it. You will not be sleep-deprived unless you "fight the flow."
4. Feeling that you are going crazy, or losing your mind. This may also feel as if you are unable to focus in the manner you are accustomed to.
5. Revisiting habits and patterns that you were confident were gone. Try not to go into judgment around this. In order to fully "ascend," you must be at peace with old habits. Just say "thank you," and keep moving forward!
6. Emotional tenderness, mood swings, and "mania." Know that you are moving an extreme amount of energy. Be gentle with yourself through this shift.
7. Embracing Unity Consciousness. Feeling overwhelming love for all of humanity, the planet, your existence.
8. Heightened sensitivity to smell, sound, and taste. This can also include a shift in your eating preferences, aromas you enjoy, and music selections.

9. Losing track of "time." This can manifest as missing appointments or exits on the freeway. Being late for meetings, needing to ask, "What day is this?"

10. Dropping or bumping into things. Be careful here! Know when it is not a good time to be cutting the vegetables!

11. "Hearing" high-pitched tones, or a series of tones. This may also be accompanied by a pressure in one or both ears.

12. Spiritual death, or brief suicidal thoughts. Try to remember that these are merely third-dimensional concepts trying to find an understanding of what you are experiencing.

13. A heightened sense of "not being on the planet." This may also express itself as a sense of detachment, and occasionally may feel like a hangover.

14. A general sense of free-floating energy that can often manifest and be misinterpreted as anxiety without basis.

15. Kriyas: Spontaneous jolts of energy that are felt physically, and often will move your body. They can be felt as waves of energy or a sudden jolt that may lift you. Breathe through this experience and let the energy flow.

16. Lack of focus and attention for any length of time. Try to be patient here, keep lists, and simply recognize that you were busy in another dimension.

17. Heightened / newfound discomfort in some public environments. This is usually triggered in "high-density" buildings with toxic lighting, air, building materials, etc.

18. Sudden urge to make everything spacious. You may desire to release a personal "treasure," feel a need to remove old clutter, donate old belongings, and remove furniture.

19. Heartburn or chest pressure. Your Galactic Heart is opening!

20. Attraction to new colors. This can also include a desire to totally change your wardrobe, paint your bedroom, etc.

21. Change of priorities in your career / relationships. This often occurs when there would be no "rational" reason to make a change; however, you feel called to make a change.

22. Feeling of "moving fast." You are energetically accomplishing more in a shorter period of time! This may be accompanied by a

physical "rush of energy" sensation. You may find yourself on a Friday feeling as if a month has passed instead of a week.

23. Sudden shifts in your perceptions. For example, you may notice that you "feel" as if all the cars on the highway are stopped, even though you are driving through them!

TIPS FOR FLOWING WITH AAEE'S

1. First and foremost, do not panic or overreact! Know that this too shall pass.

2. Offer yourself the gift of deep breathing. Bring your hand to your heart, center yourself, take a deep breath, *and trust your process!*

3. Choose Joy!

4. Drink as much fresh, pure water as you can.

5. "Lighten" your nourishment. Ascension Energy is "light," and a dense diet will be in conflict with the flow. A vegetarian diet will make the transition easier. Even if you only "lighten" a few days a week, you will notice the difference.

6. Use the Mantra of Self-Ascension daily to ground yourself in the truth of conscious evolution. *I am Here, I am Ready, I am Open, Guide me!*

7. Gift yourself with gentle movement every day. This can be as simple as walking, Sacred Yoga, swimming, etc. Just allow yourself the connection of moving the energy. There is great magnetism in the foundational energies of Density Consciousness.

Density is the degree of solidness. In a world of form, it feels stabilizing to the body. As polarity and chaos accelerate in the coming times, many people will feel called to further densify. That is, they will not have the support to assist them through the transition from Density Consciousness into Ascension Awareness.

Ascension Acceleration Energy Experiences can be uncomfortable. If you are unable to cultivate a sense of trust, and do not have a community of supporting friends, it may be very challenging to persevere through these experiences.

Eating denser foods, combined with taking medications, will offer some immediate comfort. Making a habit of these choices will generate a trend toward deeper densification. There is great magnetism in Density Consciousness. This nonverbal "pull" is a self-preserving intelligence built right into the veil.

Understanding the nature of the veil will help you make the transition out of density alignment, if that is your choice. Making the transition is indeed easier with the encouragement and support of others on the same path.

As we release our attachments to density dramas and material-world payoffs, we begin to naturally lift into the fifth dimension. Staying there is determined by our ability to reside in our Ascended Heart.

The Ascended Heart offers the foundation. From there we can lift into subtle realms and evolve increasingly refined discernments. It is a Joy to align with the "you" that is boundless. Stepping into multidimensional consciousness is usually done in baby steps, for that is all the earthbound ego can "rationally" accept.

It does take some time to integrate the new energies and discernments. You have the time between now and 2012. Why not get started?

INTERDIMENSIONAL CONTACT: STOP...LOOK...LISTEN!

You are not alone. You have never been alone. Many who are traveling with you reside on the other side of the veil. There is much support available to you if you simply call it in. Your Angels delight in offering loving energetic assistance! Just as noninterference in the physical realm is the attitude of one who holds great respect and love for another, so too will the Angels wait for you to ask before offering their assistance.

In this time of global transition, we are being prepared as gently as possible for the reunification opportunity of 2012. That is, the veil between the dimensions is thinning, and new opportunities for soul travel and soul expression lie ahead. There are Beings who reside on other planets and in other dimensions who are waiting to greet us.

"Yes, Virginia, there is intelligent life on other planets!"

These "aliens" are also experiencing their acceleration energies and being called to Reunion just as we are here on Earth. For the most part, these interdimensional Beings have a clearer understanding of galactic cosmology than we have on Earth. That is to say, their history of soul expansion did not include as many refraction[42] experiences as we have encountered on Earth. Not having the density we choose to experience, they enjoy greater conscious communion with galactic truth and will thus appear to be more advanced than we are.

The idea of "advanced" is simply a hierarchical construction of Earth consciousness. It simply does not apply once we leave this dimension. The tools for expression and travel arise with the need for them.

Many people are now feeling that they are connecting with the energies of "visitors" from other worlds or dimensions. Yes, they are! There is a lot of confusion surrounding this subject as the governments of the world have not shared all they know about the visitors. For the purposes of this book, it is especially important to understand that there are many, many, many benevolent energies that wish to make their presence known to us. Similarly, there are those that are not as benevolent, and they also want to make their presence known.

Cloud Ships offer one example of this gentle intention to connect. Using the energy of a familiar and comforting sight, clouds can be overlaid with holographic information from these visitors. That is, the Cloud Ships are energy projections that carry intelligence, intention, and information. You can communicate with these visitors through their projections. It is a way of preparing the human psyche for more direct contact, which lies not too far ahead!

This photograph *(see page 122)* was taken by us just south of Flagstaff, Arizona. The day was extremely windy, so there were no other clouds in the sky. They simply could not be still. Yet, this cloud communicated with us for several hours, and we were compelled to stop driving and say hello.

During our time of communication, we received much of the information we are sharing now. Most amazingly, with this very obvious signal in the sky, most people kept on driving by, simply not noticing.

Our galactic friends confirmed this by sharing:

Many claim to see us. Many claim to know we are here. Yet today only four have stopped to pay attention and see our presence. You two are among the four, and we also encourage you to keep listening to all that is shared, all that is coming, and all that is ready to be revealed to your world now.

P.S. We were delighted when we developed this picture and found the road sign that had a stop with an arrow, pointing up. Coincidence? Perhaps our visitors assisted us by suggesting where to pull off the road so that we could STOP, LOOK, and LISTEN.

Chapter Eleven

SAFETY, SEX, AND POWER—THE AUTHENTICITY PYRAMID

To the uninformed, chakras are taken to be mystical entities derived from Eastern traditions. While many people in the West have little understanding of chakras and their energy, these energy centers are quite real. We need to appreciate the Eastern teachers, for they have studied the subtle energies for centuries and have evolved various disciplines, or yogas, from their learning.

The word "chakra" is Sanskrit for "wheel" or "disk," and signifies one of the basic energy centers in the body. There are seven major chakras which branch forth from the spinal column *(see Figure A)*. Each of these chakras has a strong association with systems and organs of the human body, as well as with certain emotional and spiritual issues.

Chakra energies typically spin in a clockwise direction, swirling outward from the spine. They can be measured and felt. The amount and the quality of the chakra energy typically correlate with the overall health of the person, with a decline in energy in one chakra having significant consequences for the organs of the body associated with that energy center.

Most people have an intuitive understanding of the chakra energies. The crown chakra at the top of the head is the area where Divine Communion flows into the person. In ancient drawings, saints and sovereigns and others who were felt to be in communion with God are depicted with halos of golden energy floating at the top of their heads. Similar to the Angel-wings myth, these halos, or nimbuses, are the visible expressions of crown chakra energies.

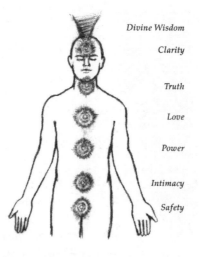

Divine Wisdom

Clarity

Truth

Love

Power

Intimacy

Safety

Figure A

We all intuitively understand that the fourth chakra, located in the center of the chest, emanates love energy. The fifth chakra, at the base of the throat, is associated with the ability to say what you mean; therefore, having laryngitis, or a sore or scratchy throat, is often related to feeling unsafe about expressing your own needs, and/or an uncomfortable truth.

The lower three chakras are rooted in the density experience. That is, there is no Ascended version of the lower chakras, while there does exist a higher-frequency alignment in the upper chakras.

The first chakra, at the base of the spine, is associated with one's grounding in the physical world and with issues of safety, self-preservation, and belonging. The second chakra, near the navel, is associated with emotion, intimacy, and sexuality. The third chakra, at the solar plexus, is associated with ego identity, personal power, and the muscular system. Each of these three chakras is identified with the body and tied to the third-dimensional density experience.

Beginning with the fourth chakra, the heart, the energies become increasingly refined. Thus, the fourth chakra is associated with the energy of love, and the fifth chakra, the throat area, with Truth. The sixth chakra, often referred to as the "third eye," is associated with mental clarity and clairvoyance. The seventh chakra opens to Divine Connectivity and wisdom.

In general, as a person evolves, they move their energetic focus up the chakra system. Thus, to a youngster finding his way in a world of grownups and uncharted environments, safety is a daily concern (first chakra). To the young adult, sexuality and intimacy are at the forefront of their experience (second chakra). Ego identity and a sense of personal power are issues commonly present in the workplace (third chakra). Of course, all chakra energies are available at all times. Thus, all can know love; all can know Divine Flow.

It usually takes some time for people to be able to access Universal Love and Divine Wisdom. The issues of the lower three chakras are simply "too compelling," and preoccupy our attention. This is why yoga and meditation are especially useful in helping us access the higher streams of energy.

To the extent that a person has unresolved emotional issues, the associated chakra will spin out energy associated with that issue. This energy is an invisible attractor to those who have similar issues. People are drawn together by their energy, and have the opportunity to work through the issues that are distorting their energy flow.

For example, often someone who has an unresolved sexual abuse history sends out a chakra energy that attracts a partner who has sexual issues as well. Similarly, a victim attracts a perpetrator and an addict finds an enabler. Each of these patterns puts out an energy signature which invites a relationship with someone who resonates with the distorted energy flow. This results in a mutual healing opportunity.

Your chakras carry your consciousness and energy out into the environment. They are lenses through which you view the world. They engage the world at the level of their song, and we call into our lives circumstances and people who offer an energetic fit, and an opportunity to bring the unresolved issues to the forefront of awareness.

The lower three chakras are completely aligned with the density experience. These three chakras are whirlpools of energy associated with traditional density understandings. These chakras will not go away because they serve to keep the body alive; they just become more peaceful as we mature and heal. As you are able to hold the energy of spaciousness and love, the energy of the lower chakras evolves from a whirlpool into the Divine infinite swirl. They quiet down, and you are then less distracted by issues of safety, sex, and power. You find it easier to center yourself in the heart if you choose to interrupt the event-response cycle with the energy of gratitude.

If you are experiencing an emotion that is not Peace, Love, or Joy, then one of your lower chakras has been activated. The key is to **breathe deeply and say thank you,** for it is in the recognition that you are not in Joy that you find your true power! No matter how evolved we might consider ourselves, from time to time events in the world will trigger an unpleasant experience. When that happens, an event-response loop has been initiated, based on an unconscious judgment or hurt that you are carrying. You have a choice as to how you will interact with the experience. Once the pain signal has caught your attention, you must decide where to go next.

It is easier to intercept an event-response loop when one brings the Ascended Heart energy to the situation. With gratitude and love in place, any pain-based event can be expanded beyond its perceived limitations. The world of experience will give you many, many, many opportunities to practice returning to your heart! Address each event with love and gratitude, and your peace will be assured.

The Self-Ascension Chakra Portrait *(see Figure B, below)* offers a visual representation of the chakras swirling in the state of Divine Completion, the infinity symbol. The lower chakras still offer energy and energetic nourishment to the physical body. However, the flow of that energy is balanced and reflects the connection of the person's consciousness with Divine Flow. It offers you a glimpse of the state sought by followers of most of the world's religious traditions, one in which the heart is swirling energy in all directions, and the transpersonal connection to All-That-Is (the Lotus Chakra) is active. The Chakra Portrait also offers a view of the golden portal of swirling spiral energy that surrounds one who is in balance and communion.

Regardless of your understanding of the chakra system, we all understand Love. We all recognize that love heals, love unifies, love encourages, love expands, love nourishes us. Nothing we have shared in this book will take you somewhere you don't want to go.

The intention of this work is to offer you an expanded paradigm and to help you anchor in your heart. It aims to assist you in recognizing the freedom that comes when you trust your heart and inner knowing. When we truly anchor in our hearts, new responses to perceived problems arise automatically. True harmony results!

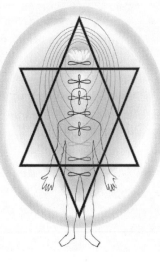

Figure B

GALACTIC YOGA PRACTICE TO
OPEN AND HARMONIZE THE CHAKRAS

This practice is a powerful opener and cleanser. It will prepare you for deeper Divine Connection. We call it the Living Ankh Practice and it was first introduced to us by Archangel Metatron.[43] Here is the transcript of this teaching.

ARCHANGEL METATRON: *There are two energy rays that enter, and it is at the chakra you call the root that the two rays unite. They must come in through the sole chakras of the feet; let us call them those for now to distinguish. Bring the two rays in through the sole chakras and up each extremity—or leg as you call it—until they become one at the root chakra, as you refer to it. Then it is important to understand that they intertwine.*

    This is most important to understand. This is the premise for all true energy shifting and work, as you would want to call it. You should open both (sole) chakras, not just the one.

SRI RAM KAA: And then they intertwine?

Yes, it is the two energies as they enter in here, through the feet. They come in as two separate rays. It is most important to understand this. This will shift a perception many have about energy and working with energy, and will bring the alignment of energy to a greater purpose.

    It is vital that when you do the Living Ankh (cross) exercise, that you start by bringing the energy in through these foot chakras, first letting them go through all the traditional chakras until back out through the crown. Then call in the emerald flame to the heart. Extending throughout the hands there are two chakras that swirl. These are most important. They are located in the lower part of the palm.

    It is important to know that these chakras of the palms are most powerful for the transmission, the giving of energy. The sole chakras, as we are referring to them now, are for receiving energy. This is why you should always start at the feet and move up, ending at the hands, so that all that has entered can also be released. Also as a worker of Light and energy, you use this portion of the hands to work with others. This simple shift in the way that energy work is performed will enhance the result tenfold.

Try this, so you may feel and see for yourself. You will notice the difference and be able to feel this. Once this is activated, it is a God-center chakra. It is the God-center chakra because it enables you to be of greatest service. It allows you to give. It allows you to fully release.

The Living Ankh exercise will open these chakras for any, but you must first have the full rays come in through the sole chakras, then up and out through the crown. Then call in the emerald flame to the heart to expand out, thereby pushing out any remnants in these chakras, for chakras are truly energy centers. This is all they are, chakra energy centers.

THE LIVING ANKH PRACTICE

This practice is done in two steps. It is important that you first run the energy up your feet and out the top of your head, and then out through your hands. Begin by standing. Visualize a white ray of light coming into your left foot and up the left leg, and visualize a golden ray of light entering your right foot and up the right leg. These rays meet at the base of your spine where they intertwine at each of the traditional chakras. This intertwining will give you the visual effect of the caduceus, an ancient symbol that has been commonly adopted by medical doctors. Send this blended energy stream all the way up and out the crown.

A typical caduceus

After you have established this energy flow from the feet up, then call in an emerald beam from the universe right into your heart chakra. Extend your arms to each side and send the energy out each arm and then out through each palm chakra.

See this green energy blend with the golden/white spiral and then ask it to flow out your palms. Extend your hands outward as far as you are able, and call in an ever-greater flow.

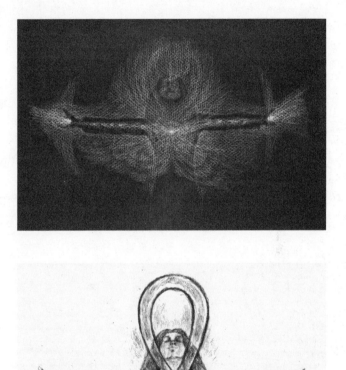

TELL ME MORE ABOUT THE ANKH

Believed by most to be Egyptian in origin, the ankh is often viewed as the first cross.

It was first used by Africans in Egypt as the symbol for life. Yet the ankh was brought here from the Atlantean experience, and was one of the energies unveiled during the Egyptian dynastic period as an Atlantean reminder.

There are numerous hieroglyphic representations of the ankh shown in the hands of ancient Egyptian deities, often handing it to the king, thereby granting eternal life. It is important to remember that this eternal life belongs to each one of us. You are the Living Ankh.

As you view the ankh, notice the loop at the top. This is the representation of eternal life, while the section at the bottom represents the material plane. The horizontal section offers the reconnection with Divine Union energy.

It was only when the ankh was brought into the Earth plane during the Egyptian era that the bottom came together as if it were a singular energy and stiffened / coagulated along with all other matter (hence, the traditional Egyptian ankh).

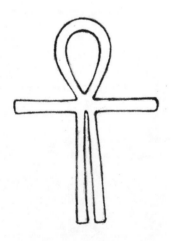

Atlantean Ankh

Egyptian Ankh

The Living Ankh of Self-Ascension translates into "eternal life." As the symbol of Self-Ascension, the bottom is split, representing the male/female polarity becoming one as unity is expressed. This opening to receive the Divine Energy restores it to its original form at the time of Atlantis.

NAVIGATING THE AUTHENTICITY PYRAMID IN FULL CONSCIOUSNESS

Many have forgotten that our essence is the canvas upon which our creations are painted. Refractions display a unifying principle once we lift our gaze from the individual pieces. Oneness, or the state of Union, is the peaceful recognition of the Divine expressing through the seeming polarity, the seeming chaos and antagonism of the world's energies. Oneness cannot be known as long as you take sides!

Taking sides, however, is a *path* toward Oneness, as long as we are awake to our decisions. Choose wisely. Choosing an action that is loving and inclusive is a wonderful expression of consciousness in action. Sometimes we must respond to what is before us. Be in trust that if your heart says "act," and you do act, you are living authentically. Participating in the world's dramas, the density creations, always means that you are seduced by a particular point of view. You cannot make the world a better place if you think something is wrong with it. Thinking something is wrong makes you a player in the game of duality, and will keep you tied to the game board of density. This tie is called attachment. Your attachments turn the wheel of reincarnation and activate karma as your choice, rather than as an imperative. This is not wrong; it is simply a choice, and part of your journey.

Remember that as long as you are attached, you can be interfered with. As long as you believe that there's something that "must be corrected" or something that you must fix, then you are entranced by the game. This is precisely what the Illuminati want, for then you voluntarily choose to return to density and offer your Divine Light to their domain. This reassures them that they "are right!" And so the game of density creation continues… The game will continue as long as you want to play. There is no way off the game board of density except through lifting—transcending the attachments that keep you bound to the density value system.

Being "very awake" is quite fun; it gives you a taste of freedom and empowerment while preserving friendships and other benefits of the game. Yet, playing the role of the Awakening One is just another role, is it not?

In each lifetime you played a role. And in each lifetime you really ("really") believed in your role, for you thought it was who you were. Your role was your identity. Perhaps it is time to transcend the personal identity and simply be a witness to the flow of all life.

So...*seek not* to be awake. *Seek not* to be enlightened.

Claim your Mastery as you claim your conscious choice to focus your attention on the Divine Energy. Be enlightened by claiming your authentic soul as Self. This is a state of Beingness that needs no proof. Your soul is already enlightened! Now, let your consciousness loosen its grip on the belief patterns and emotions that would keep you distracted from this truth.

Enlightenment is not a path. Ascension Consciousness is a state of Being in which the ego surrenders to the Unconditional Love of the Soul. Ascension Consciousness recognizes that it is not of the density world, yet finds itself here! How amusing! And shortly after the truth of that recognition is anchored without doubt, one's vibrational rate will escalate very rapidly. Yes, you will leave the world of illusion and you will find many others doing the same.

To those "left behind," it may appear as if you simply left the room! In some cases, you'll leave the body behind, appearing to have suddenly died. The choice of whether to take your body is yours too; however, there are some places that the physical body cannot go. If you decide to venture to those realms, you'll gratefully cast aside the heaviness of the physical vehicle.

Ascension is the process of lifting out of the density realm. Many will choose to ascend once they drop the body. Self-Ascension is the process of doing this by conscious choice, while still in the body.

Re-Union is available to all, yet not everyone is ready. Some have their consciousness so fixed on other explorations and beliefs that they are not available to this gateway to Oneness. Each soul finds its own way home, and in its own perfect time; that is the nature of free will. Just as children might miss the call to dinnertime due to their intense involvement in a game, so too will millions voluntarily opt out of this opportunity for reunion. This is not a loss; rather, it is merely a choice to stay out and play longer.

The universe is infinitely patient. Yet there is urgency. We are at the time of reunion. The dawn of 2012 offers energetic support for this call home. The timing is supportive; your success is assured!

Are you ready to take the steps required to Self-Ascend? Ready to take the steps through the distractions, the enticements, and the values that would keep you earthbound? We look forward to welcoming you home.

When we allow ourselves to stabilize and accept ourselves in balanced recognition through authenticity, we can further unveil the Pyramid of Spiritual Awakening in relation to our experiences at the current time on the planet.

We refer to this as the Authenticity Pyramid *(see next page)*. Within this pyramid, each stratum of consciousness previously revealed in the Pyramid of Spiritual Awakening now illuminates energy that, when expressed, opens authentic channels of Divine recognition within. This is especially potent for those energies known as emotions that our mind may seek to judge as not optimum to experience. Through the journey of authenticity, these emotions become relevant in our journey toward wholeness, and are powerfully symbolic as we speed toward 2012.

You are here, on this planet AND at this moment in history, to remember the truth of who you are. By opening yourself to full acceptance of this truth, the Pyramid of Spiritual Awakening, expressed through the lens of authenticity, naturally expands as follows:

Density Consciousness = Apathy/Attachments

Spiritual Activism = Anger/Action

Ascension Awareness = Acceptance of Allness

Ascension Consciousness = Allness Awakened into Oneness

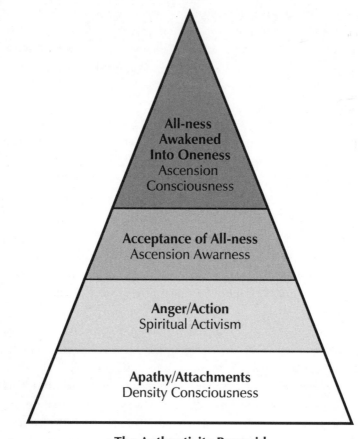

The Authenticity Pyramid
©2008 Sri Ram Kaa and Kira Raa

Perhaps you have navigated your own authenticity through all of the levels presented above in any one given moment of a situation. It is valuable to offer yourself the gift of taking this moment to stop, breathe fully, and simply be in integrity with yourself.

As you gaze at this pyramid, where does your authenticity express most often? Does life often make you angry? Do the actions of others spark action within you? If so, then you are responding authentically as a spiritual activist. Celebrate this recognition.

Most importantly, are you able to love yourself through this self-inquiry? Awakening your authenticity is the giant step toward the 2012 experience of humanity, and you can do it… In fact, you already are.

Chapter Twelve

TALK TO ME ABOUT KARMA

Karma (definition): The quality of somebody's current and future lives as determined by that person's behavior in this and in previous lives.

When revealing the imminence of 2012, it becomes imperative to acknowledge another moment in our collective history that occurred just a few years ago. Many are unaware that this event occurred, yet it was a powerful and highly influential event that did not make the front page of the paper or the evening news.

At the millennium, while millions were preparing for a Y2K computer calamity by storing water and food, the universe was joyously offering us all a great gift. Yes, there was a mighty "blast" that hit our planet at the millennium. It was a blast of grace so powerful that it has forever positively shifted our opportunities to consciously co-create.

This event was not noticed by most because their attention was turned elsewhere. While the world focused on making a living and planning for Y2K dramas, the universe offered humanity a tremendous gift—the full release of the karmic imperative. And we did not even notice!

OK. Breathe, turn off your cell phone, grab a cup of tea, and just be present. You really need to take this in:

THE KARMIC IMPERATIVE HAS BEEN RELEASED

Why is the realization of the release of the karmic imperative [44] so alarming? Because it means that the playing field has changed. What would change in your life now if you knew there was no karmic imperative to bind you? What if you were fully responsible, right now, for your experience of the now?

Indeed, it is the last question that elicits the greatest response. When Archangel Zadkiel revealed this amazing information, we immediately knew it was important to share with as many people as possible.

Many want to cling to their beloved karma, and the awesome news is, they can! Only now, it is their choice. For those aligned with Eastern traditions, the concept of karmic debt is similar to Christian penance; it's seen as the causative and transformational repository for any and all misfortune. The release of the karmic imperative means that all debts are forgiven, all contracts are complete, and everyone is free to be fully responsible for their actions, here and now. This is a tremendous shift in consciousness IF you allow it in. With this freedom comes great responsibility and great Joy.

Imagine our surprise when the editor of a "progressive" metaphysical paper would not publish our article unless we agreed to remove the revelation of the karmic release. "That is simply too much for my readers to accept," was the publisher's declaration.

Her assumption that "people" did not want to accept the release of the karmic imperative was for us a great gift. We saw that *the habit of the habit of the pain of the pain* [45] is indeed a universal veil that had obscured her willingness to challenge her belief structures. Needless to say, as we cannot rescind what we know to be true, we rescinded the article.

KARMA IS A CHOICE!

The most powerful time of co-creation is upon us now. You can continue in the habit of feeling indebted, constrained, or compelled, or you can become responsible right now. In this moment you can claim self-responsibility for everything in your experience.

Karma has become a habitual orientation. To be free, one must recognize that karma is now a limiting belief and accept its release. Expansion is different from cycling through the same energy over and over again. Recognition of the release of the karmic imperative frees us all from the repetitive cycle! Alternatively, you can choose to engage your co-creative power to stay focused on the wheel of karma and disregard the power of the present moment.

ARCHANGEL ZADKIEL EXPLAINED THIS AS FOLLOWS:

QUESTIONER: What is the fastest way out of the trap of feeling that we must pay karma in order to achieve total liberation?

ARCHANGEL ZADKIEL: *Good question! We have much to say about karma. Okay. Remember Y2K? At the time of Y2K, all that was karma, all the ways of the old, and all the ways of the third-dimensional energy ended. This was the blowup everybody was waiting for! You see, dearest ones, there is no karma. Not anymore! It is gone.*

Many will say, "You've got to be kidding me!"

No, we are not! We are very serious! We are not kidding you! What is left since the time of the millennium release and the energetic and vibrational shift on the planet is—habit. It is the habit of the habit, of the pain of the pain that lets you believe that you are still bound in a karmic connection. There is no karma, dearest ones. This is why your chakras are free to lift. This is why you can now embrace living in the Ascended Root, the center of the heart. This is why the first, second, and third chakras can be relegated to what they are there for, to simply help you hold onto a body until you can say, "Been there, done that, don't need it anymore!"

So, the easiest way to release third-dimensional habit and pain is to accept that there is no more karmic connection. There is only the habit of reinforced belief patterns which, while very strong, can be easily released by going into the heart center and living in the Ascended State. This understanding requires re-training of the body. So too, learning to live in the heart center is a training.

It is important to understand that the ways that were perfect prior to Y2K are the ways that helped you evolve. They're the beliefs that helped you pave the way to who you are now. You were all lifted as this dimension shifted into the time of the rapid escalation, and it will get even more rapid, oh yes! As you shifted into this time, you were given the grace of release from that pattern of energy (karma), so that you could be free to receive the new energies. Your cellular memory knows this or you would not be here, on this planet, now.

QUESTION: I have a question about karma because you have said that with the arrival of the millennium, karma was over. I want to understand the things that are happening right now. Is it a cleanup? When you hear of things that happened in situations, is the past-life pull actually over in those situations? I just need you to address the karmic issue a little more.

ARCHANGEL ZADKIEL: *It is a powerful question that you ask, and many seek to understand this better. Yes, all karma, as you understand karma, was lifted off of this planet during the time of the millennium. This was a predetermined timing that is part of the expansionary experience.*

It is the time when the recycling of lifetimes and the learning of soul lessons is transmuting from a density-based system of alignment. You are now free to embrace reunification energy. Now we must go back and explain what we just said, do we not?

Those of light who have been on this journey have been traveling for a very long time. The goal, if you would use the word goal, of light is to experience, to expand, and become ever more joyous. As light, you recreate continually, often becoming within yourself greater light, greater being-ness, greater color, greater tone, greater harmony. With every cycle you have become more refined, more open, and available to more.

We talk now just about the third cycle,[46] for indeed you have cycled through this expression three times. In this third cycle of the experience of light as density, in this culminating time, on this planet, you have gone through many different soul evolutions. You have also had many experiences that were not on THIS planet. Yet, you have touched this planet at least more than once, which is why you are asking this question now.

For many years great wisdom has been revealed that offered you the opportunity to break free of karmic cycles. However, up until this time, very few have broken free. And because there have been so few, you point to them and say, look at this one, look at that one. You call them masters, you call them prophets; you call them many things. They have indeed shown many paths to relief or release through that cycle. Yet as great beings of light, you are all "predestined," in the words again of this world, to reunify.

You are at the time now. Visualize a big ball. You have been moving all the way around the ball and now you are ready to slingshot your way back. This is the only way we can describe that. YES, it is hyperdrive. It is indeed!

As you are ready to return to reunification, it is no longer a karmic debt. There is nothing to be repaid on either a personal, if you use this word, or a global basis. Everything now is part of reunification, everything!

We offer you the word "densi-full." In an energy that is very densi-full, there are great habits that say things can only be happening because of karmic debt. There are those who refuse to believe that karma is lifted, so indeed they will continue the habitual patterning that creates it. Yet, it can be gone in a twinkling, in the very moment of recognition.

The energy of karmic repayment is gone. The time of the Ascended Chakras is available to you now. None of these energies were available on the planet until the time of the karmic release, which happened at the millennium.

You are rapidly entering a cycle. How many of you feel that days now seem like hours? Does not time seem like it has sped up so much you cannot keep up with it? Guess what, don't! [much laughter] We encourage you to let go of linear time. It will make you crazy. You will look at your watch and go, "How did this happen? Cannot be! What day is it?" You will find yourself doing this more and more. Those who do stay closely aligned to linear time without recognition will indeed find themselves in greater discomfort.

We understand that you are living in a world that places restrictions on you. You say, "I must be here at a certain time; I must be there at a certain time." OK, recognize that, without being it. Do not own it.

When you have days without scheduled time, train yourself to let go of all time. Get up when you need to get up. Go to sleep when you need to go to sleep. Just because so many say it is the correct way to do something, if your heart knows different, trust your heart. Start training your heart. Start training your heart.

Like so many of Archangel Zadkiel's teachings, this discourse gives us the opportunity to embrace a new understanding about the universe, karma, and the time ahead. Sometimes Zadkiel guides the audience in a practice that helps integrate the energy of what was just shared. We strongly recommend that you reread the preceding teaching and then do the next practice.

PRACTICE

ARCHANGEL ZADKIEL: *Begin with your right hand on your heart. With the hand on your heart, allow yourself to understand the truth of the root chakra of the Ascended State. Close your eyes, feeling the energy in the swirl of the Divine symbol of infinity. Feel the crystalline emerald green of this symbol. Know it as it comes through you.*

Expand this so that it goes beyond your body, beyond your city, beyond this planet. Send out this energy. You can do it; you know how. As you send it out and expand it, call in the infinity symbol that interlocks with this one. It is the vibrant pure gold. Vertically interlocking with this one (the emerald green), allow that vibrant gold to go up, all the way up and out the crown.[47]

Now send it all the way down and out your feet. Let the two become one. Let it clear and heal your emotional and physical body. Let it escalate your vibration. This is the truth of this practice. This is the place of spacious energy.

Relax and release your arm from your heart as we ask you to bring both hands down to the solar plexus to do some further cleansing. With your hands on your solar plexus,[48] call in that same heart symbol of the integrated infinite, the emerald infinite with the gold infinite interlocked. Let it embrace all of what used to be there.[49] Yes, breathe again. Call in the linkage and let it release. This is a powerful gift! Breathe ever deeper . . . out, in again, out, in, and out. Relax your hands outwards and say thank you to yourself! Thank you, thank you, and you may relax.

You may also wish to try this exercise just before retiring in the evening. We have found it to be most centering and restful. Often we experience deep rest and positive dream space when we practice just before bed. It is also a wonderful couples practice. Simply face each other and maintain eye contact while you share this heart-opening exercise.

So what does the Archangelic Realm have to offer about these plasmic goodies? When we asked, we received an answer that made perfect

Understanding Orbs and Why They Are Here

Orbs! What are these mysterious and most wondrous balls of light that are appearing in so many pictures these days? There are many different opinions about these mystical light emanations. We have noticed that, without exception, the majority of photographs we take at every event have numerous orbs in them.

sense. We are at a time of undeniable contact with many dimensions, worlds, and energies. Every day, more and more of the veil is thinning to offer us glimpses of the fifth-dimensional world and beyond, thereby gently preparing our sensitive nervous systems.

Think about it—just a few years ago the idea of an orb appearing in your photos was not even in your consciousness. Now they appear with great regularity and are becoming more and more common, especially among gatherings of individuals who are calling forth the loving energies of the universe.

In any setting, they are a true gift. We like to call them "Angel Hearts," as they frequently appear in photos when there is an atmosphere of Joy or Love. Orbs offer loving proof that interdimensional energies are present with us at all times. Each time an Angel Heart appears in our pictures, it reminds us that we are being prepared for a true shift in our consciousness, and that we are loved so much that we are being given this time of gradual adjustment.

The next time an Angel Heart appears in your pictures, remember that you are being asked to look into another dimension. The veil is not as thick as it may seem, and is getting thinner all the time.

Thousands seek to see on the other side, and yet the more profound truth is that their central nervous system is simply not ready. Many would have an immediate heart attack from the shock of the direct contact that they believe themselves ready for. When we expand beyond our ego and brain orientations, we can then recognize that we are being lovingly acclimatized to seeing beyond our singular world through these lovely energies we call orbs.

Orbs are now expanding in nature beyond the common form shown in the photos printed here; most likely you have seen or taken more elaborate ones yourself. On our ranch in New Mexico, the extraordinary amount of documented orb phenomena has attracted TV crews, documentary filmmakers, and visitors from all over the world. Why?

We are fully open to this expression of multidimensional experience, and joyously celebrate the communion. A safe energetic environment is thereby created for these gifts of the universe to be shared with many.

One such event was the presence of an energy portal appearing in the following photographs. During one of our monthly gatherings, we celebrated a ley line[50] activation on our property, and then many gathered to walk the spiral labyrinth around our giant Merkabah.

Photo A

Filled with Love and Joy, the events in these candid photos were captured seconds apart (note the positions of those walking the labyrinth), yet in Photo B, a portal "magically" appears.

A first we suspected that perhaps this was just a bird, or some other flying object in the sky, yet there was no evidence in the first photo (A) of anything entering the area. Upon closer inspection (Photo C), we noticed that the portal has a hollow center and is certainly not a bird or other object. The "orb" is indeed proof of a portal to multidimensional space, visible through loving intention.

Photo B

Photo C

How does your brain receive this information? This is the important question to ask yourself, and is the primary reason for the appearance of orbs: to lovingly prepare us to receive greater information without shocking our nervous systems. A glorious gift.

Chapter Thirteen

MANIFESTING
RESPONSE-ABLE ACTIONS

ARCHANGEL ZADKIEL: *You are eternally shifting, moving, and creating anew: over and over and over again. What a gift, the ability to continually expand. This is a process that cannot be terminated, for you cannot terminate expansion! It can only renew itself. Know that when you feel as if you are in a phase when you are not expanding, you are renewing!*

We are here to explain the creationism energy that has now expanded on the planet.

The purpose of spiritual practice is to consciously connect with the soul (you). This gift offers clarity, expansion, and connection with your authentic expression as light. Even though we yearn for Ascension, we are surrounded by Density Consciousness. Within the confines of density, it is common to be unaware of the miracles that regularly manifest before us.

WHEN DID WE BECOME A SOCIETY IN WHICH EVERYDAY MIRACLES ARE NO LONGER ENOUGH?

Commonly, we reiterate historic miracles with great awe. Often they are utilized to authenticate the divinity of a teacher or being—for example, Jesus walking on water, or changing the water into wine. Within your consciousness are several stories floating just behind your awareness. Take a moment to connect with these miracle stories now.

Letting go of the magical miracles, consider for a moment how many lives are saved through loving attention. Even the more unusual and stunning miracles are still happening today, and with ever greater frequency and intensity... We are just not paying attention to them! When we do choose to acknowledge a miracle, often there arises a need for proof or a scientific explanation (a form of Density Consciousness).

Aligned with scientific theory, this skepticism is also a by-product of fear. Many miracles today go largely unreported. This is usually due to either reverence for the event, or fear of ridicule.

Miracles have long been associated with mysticism, along with particular geographic locations and perceived sources. Yet, is not the abundant stream of conscious awakening a miracle in itself? When was the last time you remembered that YOU are a miracle?

Consider the miracle of beauty. And what about the miracle of birth? How often do you encounter or read about those who have had near-death experiences, and the subsequent gift of soul recognition upon returning to their body? Miraculous too are the severe car accidents in which, for no logical reason, everyone escapes unharmed.

We are at the time when anyone who chooses to can ascend into higher realms of consciousness. No longer does this require years of meditation in a cave or monastery. For years we have revered the revelations of mountain yogis, beings who occasion miracles through their methods of Divine Connection. A miracle is a point of view that unlocks expectation, thus our delight in magic and illusion.

What if you could delight in everything you behold? What if you could focus your intent and call upon your alignment with the universe to shift a habit pattern? Would that be a miracle?

All beings can access the gift of galactic reconnection through the heightened vibrational state that is being showered upon the planet now. In this supportive energy, we are able to bring forth the true Galactic Yoga[51] of multidimensional existence.

Many ask, "Will this time ever end? Will these energies ever be easier to live with?"

The Archangelic Realm has told us that the rapid vibratory escalation must continue. We are all being called home. If the experience of Ascension Acceleration Energies *(see page 125)* is becoming increasingly uncomfortable, then it is even more necessary to enter into integration of the energy through these Galactic Yoga practices.

While these practices may seem new to us at this time in our evolutionary existence, they were once prevalent during the Atlantean existence. It is imperative to remember that the choices made at the end-time of Atlantis directly affected the culmination of that time. The choices being made right now, in this moment, will similarly impact our collective consciousness and our collective outcome.

Miracles take many forms. Allow yourself to embrace your Divine birthright to create miracles. This creation is simply the positive flow of enhanced energy, combined with Divine Intent.

ARCHANGEL ZADKIEL: *Floating is an important energy! Try this in your bathtub. While your tub may not be big enough to fully float, it is important for you to practice the understanding of what it feels like to float, to be, to touch the Truth of the Soul. Floating is an important practice as it helps one find the depth of the Truth, and the understanding of what Truth is.*

When you float, the ego has no control.

In that moment there is you, and there is the floating. While floating, there is preciousness, vitality, Oneness, wholeness, and the truth of the being that you are.

This buoyancy is effervescent and joyous.

In this space you are open to the highest source, working through the Divine, and aligned with the Truth.

We have introduced floating as part of the gift of lifting up, healing up! It is time for you to say "Yes" to your fifth-dimensional existence while saying thank you to the hologram of this dimension. KNOW that you are the observer as you are the observed! This is an important discernment for you to remember. Let us talk to you about the next chakra of the Ascended State.

SRI RAM KAA: So, with the lower three chakras at peace, the root chakra of the Ascended State is the heart, formerly the fourth chakra. Then the Ascended Second Chakra would be the former fifth, or throat?

THE "TRUTH" CHAKRA

Yes. The second chakra in the Ascended State of Universal Oneness is the chakra of Truth. The chakra of Truth exists right now where you know the throat. This is very ironic, is it not, because it is used for much more than the Truth! Very often it is misused. Yes!

Take your hands and bring them to your throat. Let the spine go as straight as you can manage for this moment. Close your eyes and give yourself the gift of reconnecting with the emerald green spiral from your Ascended Heart.

Breathe in, and lift this spiral to your throat. Feeling the spiral lift into the throat, allow it to become sapphire blue in color. Breathe as it changes from emerald to sapphire, deep sapphire. As it does, if you feel congestion in the throat, let it come out. If you need to make noise, let it go, clear it. Let it go and relax. Float again.

We encourage you to repeat this practice again and again, and again, over a period of one month. Each time you do, you may find more caught in your throat, and even develop a sore throat.

Have you been speaking things that are not of the highest? You may be feeling things that surprise you. You may be thinking, "Why have I said that? How have I said that? How could I let myself be that way?"

Good! It is good for you to recognize what you are clearing out. It is then that you are coming into the power of the chakra of Truth! You must convert this chakra to the chakra of Truth.

RELEASING THE WORD

As you integrate and bring in the Truth, and as you integrate the new "root" which is the heart, you can come into your true center at any time. Allow the Ascended Heart Energy to lift into the Truth chakra. Remember, it is a beautiful emerald color, converted into a sapphire spiral.

The reason we say emerald converted into sapphire is that it carries aquamarine energy. It is sapphire blue with the green melded into it. This is the best we can describe this chakra. The rainbow palette of the twelve Ascended Chakras that are coming in for you now are very different from the colors you are accustomed to experiencing in density.

Now that you have brought truth energy into the throat, it is time to let go of the word. The time of wordless recognition is here. This is why you must clear the throat on all levels.

Living in the world while not being governed by the energy of Density Consciousness requires alignment with our authentic energy, our soul. This involves a shift in priorities from ego-based constructions to soul-based reality. The ego cannot prevail in all matters or you will remain anchored in the third-dimensional experience. Living in the fifth dimension involves a release of fear and a great trust in your divinity, or soul.

The practices we share throughout this book will help you to align more fully with your authentic energy. As you more closely align, your attention and your choices become more congruent. You will simply find it natural to know what is aligned with your good and what is not. Lifting into your Ascended Heart comes more easily.

To continue your alignment, you must be free of self-deception and fear in your spoken and written word as well. Ask yourself often, "Do my words align with my truth? Am I empowering false beliefs through my words? Am I feeling the judgment and expectations of others, and thus saying one thing while doing or thinking another?" In essence: "Do my words align 100% with the truth of me?"

Instead of using words for persuasion, or self-denial, or self-aggrandizement, use the word to expand Truth. Zadkiel calls the throat chakra the Truth chakra. If you open this chakra to the truth of you, your heart energy will effortlessly connect to your higher centers of consciousness.

If there is lack of will or trust, then the pathway is blocked, and you will be pulled into Density Consciousness. An aligned Truth chakra will allow the energy of your heart to connect with the crown chakra, thus fully opening your fifth-dimensional clarity.

THE TIME OF CULMINATION

ARCHANGEL ZADKIEL: *As a being of true light, all you can do is expand!*

You have been experiencing a birth cycle as beings of expansion, as beings of light. This has been a process for you for many, many, many, what you call years. This process has also been refining itself throughout three distinct cycles of density evolution. You are in the culminating time of the third cycle of the density experience.

This is the time of culmination for the expression of expansion by birthing into vessels. It is the third full expression of light, expanding through density, and the last time that you will do it this way!

You've collectively been here, done this, before. Together, you have once again attained connection with your own creationism energy.

THE EXPRESSION OF CONSCIOUSNESS

The creationism energy that has anchored into the planetary sphere has been offering rapid growth and rapid terror, rapid chaos and rapid unity, to many people. It is a time when your consciousness is being called forth as your primary expression.

You cannot hide from this. Know that with this energy fully present, your words are meaningless, and in fact have no meaning!

In an effort to call in greater consciousness, many of you speak many good words. You know the words to say but then you go home and don't live them. In the time of the calling out of the consciousness, in this time of creationism, only your absolute truth will express and manifest.

Observe as you are observed during this time. All those who are connected with you in your experience—your families, your friends, your coworkers, even those you do not know or someone you met a long time ago—all those who are connected with you in one realm or another are in this creationism process with you at this time. Therefore, all six billion beings are coming forth in the creationism energy now.

In creationism energy, the truth of your consciousness IS your expression. Your words need no validation.

As your consciousness comes into greater voice, pay attention to your life. Pay attention to your environment. Pay attention to that which you think is happening to you, for you, with you, among you. It is all an expression of the truth of your consciousness.

Here is the gift. You have the opportunity because you are aware to pay attention and ask yourself these questions:

"Do I, or do I not, need to shift my consciousness? Am I, or am I not, being true to myself?

Am I, or am I not, living the Truth? Am I speaking the Truth? Am I being the Truth?

Am I in absolute Oneness with this powerful creationism energy?"

From your answers to these questions, you may then declare with truth:

"I am aligned with divinity! I am light! I have the opportunity to call forth now the greatest form of creationism ever available, ever!"

Pay attention to every minute, every second. Observe the second within the second, and everything you do.

Keep your eyes focused on the Divine at all times! Call in consciousness.

MIRACLES ARE HAPPENING NOW!

Remember, consciousness is escalating rapidly. Pay attention! Wake up each morning with gratitude. Look in the mirror and be in Joy. All is abundantly clear; all is abundantly ready. You have eagerly awaited this time in your history; do not waste it. You can if you wish—we just suggest that you don't.

QUESTIONER: I'm wondering how to use miracles to heal relationships and help keep things clear, especially at this time. Is there anything you can offer about that?

ARCHANGEL ZADKIEL: *We appreciate your question about this time. It is important for you to understand this. All that has been, has been practice for you as beings of expansion to prepare for this time now. The greatest gift you can give is your consciousness, your awareness of consciousness, and to release the egoic bonds to relationship. Anything that ties you to relationship is egoic.*

First and foremost, go into the heart center of the relationship—and you must, all of you. If you are questioning a relationship—whether it is relationship with self or relationship with a family member or a business associate or with whomever—go to your heart first and ask, "Is this relationship for my ego, or is this relationship for my true path, my true spirit?"

Know in the moment the answer. That very first yes or no, the one you want to deny, is the true answer. It will come in right away, and from there you hold the consciousness.

Remember to watch that which is manifesting around you. Be honest, be truthful. Watch what is manifesting around you, because it is the state of your consciousness that is manifesting. Pay attention. Many blessings.

Know how loved you are. Know how revered you are.

Know how honored you are. Love yourself enough to say:

"I am ready, I am willing, and I am moving forward. I know the truth of my heart.

I know the truth of my soul, and I pay attention to the first yes! Or the first no!

I am willing to observe and I am observed. I am a beacon, and I am grateful."

DO I HAVE TO BE A VEGETARIAN
TO RAISE MY CONSCIOUSNESS?

If you wish to consciously accelerate your vibration and quickly move through the barriers in your own consciousness, then it is best to eat lightly. An organic, vegetarian diet makes good sense. It offers optimum nutrition while eliminating toxins. When you offer this pure, simple food to the body, it will automatically start cleaning out the accumulation of impurities from your previous eating habits.

THE KEY IS TO STOP EATING AND START NOURISHING

It seems that the pursuit of healthy, vitamin-rich, pesticide-free food is an expensive alternative in North America. The fact remains that mass-produced food is contaminated with chemicals, sugars, preservatives, and other additives.

The human body can handle a lot of abuse. It is a marvelous creation and it will faithfully serve you to the best of its ability. However, the modern diet offers the same dynamic and results as driving a car with the emergency brake on! It will slow you down, weigh you down, tire you out, and result in expensive repairs!

In order to raise your vibrational rate you do not have to be a vegetarian. However, it is a lot easier to anchor the new frequencies if you are! It is more loving to nourish your body with foods that do not require extra energy to process. Begin by replacing the word "eating" with the word "nourishing." From there, your awareness and your food choices will naturally shift.

In summary, we have found these steps to be the easiest way to transmute density diseases while also raising your vibratory level:

1. Listen to your body. Offer it loving presence and gratitude.
2. Eat organic foods, primarily vegetables.
3. Drink two to three quarts of pure water daily.
4. Learn to safely fast and cleanse your body with fresh air and sunlight.
5. Rest well. Clear out all clutter from around your sleeping space.

6. Consciously call in your Divine Connection through prayer, meditation, yoga, etc.

7. Choose Joy—be in a positive frame of mind!

> Gratitude is the natural state of an open
> heart, a simple allowing of Divine Love
> that comes with the conscious recognition
> of flow.
>
> Gratitude is the natural attitude of one who
> is connected with Divine Love.
>
> ~SRI RAM KAA

Connection with Divine Energy is an opportunity to share consciousness with all and to recognize that the Allness is not limited to this planet, solar system, or galaxy. When you allow yourself to expand beyond the limiting beliefs of Density Consciousness, an opening to greater love and acceptance is found. We are connected to realms beyond this planet.

Embracing the Galactic Yogic traditions as being revealed from the Archangelic Realm offers an energetic stream of connection similar to an exchange on a telephone. Essentially, you begin a transmission that is saying, "We are awake, and we are ready to reunify."

It is always optimal to begin each day, or at least each Galactic Yogic practice, with the Star Practice. The Star Practice is the precursor to all multidimensional travel and invites a state of being that opens dormant DNA strands while maintaining a balanced emotional, physical, and spiritual body. This practice should be mastered prior to integration of the rest of the practices!

THE STAR PRACTICE[52]

(The instructions given for this exercise call for a partner. Your partner should sit opposite you, and your knees should be touching your partner's knees. If you do not have a partner to practice with, then simply sit in front of a mirror and enjoy the experience.)

With your eyes open and your hands held together in prayer position, relax and focus your gaze just above the third eye (center of forehead) of your partner. Your hands are in front of your heart chakra with your thumbs touching the center of your chest, and your fingers pointed outward.

Start by imagining a glowing beautiful star on this area of the forehead. As you feel into your star, allow yourself to send the brilliant loving energy into the star of the other person. While radiating this brilliant energy, allow the words "I love you, I know you, I honor your divinity" to float on your thoughts.

Your loving energy will open your partner's star and help them to remember their own authenticity. This exercise is a focusing of love on the other, and especially helpful if you are in an uncomfortable situation. You can do the Star Practice silently whenever you find yourself confronting a challenging person or situation. Be in your Ascended Heart and beam unconditional acceptance to each other.

The Star Practice has other applications as well. It is a centering exercise that is quick and beneficial. When you practice this alone, it also provides grounding in your authenticity and promotes a habit of peaceful, loving feelings. This can also be done with an animal as a practice partner, or simply to engage the healing energy with a loved companion.

WHAT IS STAR CONSCIOUSNESS?

As most on the planet are former Atlanteans, there was a time when we accepted the great gift of Star Consciousness. Some of you may even be wondering if you are a former Atlantean.

If you are reading this book, then you are either a former Atlantean, or you were aligned with the energy that was unlocked from the original Atlantean experience during the ancient Egyptian dynasties. Often, the answer is that you were present for both. Another common trait among Atlanteans is an attraction to dolphins, Angels, crystals, and harmonic or "Angelic" music.

When the end-time of the original Atlantis was at hand, many of the galactic citizens decided that they wanted to be sure to recognize one another if and when a critical time arose in the next expression of density. Fully aware that they were Divine Light traveling as expansion, they knew that being together again was not a question. However, with the increase in density, recognizing one another would be the challenge.

Star Consciousness is an energy imprint that very much resembles a star just above your third eye in your forehead. This is why the Star Practice is so powerful. When you reconnect with this energy, it is more than just a peaceful stream of love to assist you in navigating the now. It is a gift of recognition, and one that is yours to fully embrace again.

Indeed, the time of critical action has arisen in our experience of density. We are all being called to fully participate in our co-creative process to determine how we will shift into the next experience. Claiming your Star Consciousness is a step along the path that will reawaken many talents, skills, and valuable insights into your own soul's evolution and purpose.

While many crave the experience of mystical Siddhis,[53] (visions, levitation, invisibility, etc.), the reality is such that most are not ready to accept the responsibility of the opening experience. Consider this scenario:

It is the middle of the night and you are comfortably asleep. Suddenly, you awake and there is "someone" standing in your bedroom. You are sure that you do not know this person. You can't quite make out the face and features. In that instant, your heart is racing, your adrenaline is pumping, and reactivity is flaring. What do you do now?

The bottom line is that you may panic or experience physical distress. You may react according to your inner response mechanism. It takes time to integrate multidimensional sight. The body must be trained, and you must cultivate a willing and open mind. This is one of the reasons why sincere preparation and dedicated training is suggested for all. One must not only unplug from Density Consciousness; one must gain mastery of multidimensional states of consciousness.

Now before you say "not me," take in an honest breath and relax. For many, whether this includes you or not, the truth of otherworldly experience is quite different from the fantasy. Collectively, we have been most comfortable in the belief pattern that everything we desire and fear will happen rather than that it is happening. Once you are anchored in love, even when asleep, very little will shake you.

The messages from the Archangelic Realm are all offered as gifts of preparation. Whether we care to recognize them or not, the information has still entered into our stream of consciousness. Through that stream, all can be accessed, and with the escalated planetary vibration, access to direct communication with other realms is not only possible, but is here, right now.

As with all other new forms of communication, when you are first introduced to it, you must learn how to properly use it. There are those who need to know how a cell phone works, and there are those who simply need to know that it does work. Regardless of your own need-to-know predisposition, galactic communication begins with us.

Yes, with us. As beings from the realm of deepest density, it is with great respect and love that we have been allowed to mature at our own pace. We have now reached the moment of growth that provides the opportunity to literally phone home! All extraterrestrials would be proud.

Every moment of every day on this planet, energy is being released without any concern as to its impact. This occurs on many levels, and the largest contributor is the human being. Emotional interactions release energy as part of the event-response loop.[54] Regardless of whether the release of energy is positive or negative, an impact is still made. Free-floating anxiety will attach itself to the next available event, thus tightening the event-response loop.

All released energy bonds with itself collectively as it surrounds this planet. We are at the time of conscious recognition in which we can demonstrate our awakening by responsibly recycling this energy and releasing it into the galactic stream of consciousness for reuse.

ARCHANGEL ZADKIEL SPEAKS: *It is the time to make new acquaintances. When you make an acquaintance, you create a new opening. This opening creates an energetic pattern that allows energies to meet, recognize, integrate, and be. This is the flow for all energetic shifts, and you begin by making an acquaintance.*

UNDERSTANDING CHAOTIC ENERGY

Energy is abundantly available to you. It is not a missing link; it is not something that comes in from afar. When you make an acquaintance, it is an important recognition, because not all energy should be integrated. Not all energy is for everyone. There are many different energy patterns: some are substantial, some are good for your growth, some are necessary for all paths, and some are quite unnecessary!

Abundant chaotic and scattered energies are gathered now on your planet. Think about it. What happens to energy that you discharge through day-to-day interaction? Recall now one event when you discharged energy. It may have been a reaction during driving, or your response to someone you were speaking with.

Often your body will acknowledge that there has been a chaotic energetic discharge through a physical reaction, such as butterflies in the stomach, shortness of breath, or anxiousness. Your mind will also begin a focus pattern on the chaotic discharge by "re-living" the incident, causing it to actually generate more energy!

Imagine how powerful the scattered energies are when there is a large release due to earthquakes, storms, wars, and other catastrophic events. Where does all that scattered energy go?

THE EARTH IS FULL

For many years, this energy has gathered in many different areas of your world and re-expresses itself based upon where and how it collects. Some is sent back into the Mother Gaia[55] herself, to be transmuted. Some collects in large vortexes of swirling negativity, which then birth even greater chaotic exchanges in those areas, and a lesser amount is transmuted through bliss.

You have reached the time in your collective history when you must recognize that your blessed Mother Gaia is full. Your loving planet has no choice but to stop accepting more and more chaotic energies. The vortexes of accumulated negativity must be responsibly released! It is time to demonstrate your light expansion by recognizing this need, and learning how to collectively send this energy back to those who can recycle it.

As you begin to responsibly recycle the scattered energies of this world, you will enjoy the vibration of the planet becoming ever more buoyant. We wish to offer you the Galactic Yogic Practice to recycle energy for yourself, for the planet, and beyond.

This practice should be taught to as many as possible, as it is able to quickly and joyously clear any energetic imprint. You can use it to clear imprints from a past life, from this life, on behalf of others, and, most importantly, on behalf of your world. We simply call this the Divine Container Exercise.

THE IMPORTANCE OF ENERGETIC DISCERNMENT

Understand the reason you need the Divine Container Exercise is because energies that do not suit you will inadvertently, and sometimes deliberately, attach and become a part of you. This exercise clears that which is no longer necessary, or that which does not serve, and then responsibly recycles it for use in other worlds and dimensions.

Sometimes you open up to these scattered energies when making an acquaintance without realizing or recognizing that you are welcoming in that which does not serve you. Yet, there is perfection in this. The more you welcome in that which does not serve, the quicker you learn to dispel it. It is most critical that when this energy is dispelled, it is responsibly released. This creates the gift of energetic discernment.

There are many who take on energies and hold onto them as their own without understanding that they can release them effortlessly. Through this holding, they manifest tumors, depression, illness, and other diseases of the physical body needlessly. When one feels out of balance, when one feels anything other than Peace, Love, and Joy, the first step should be to send to the container the unneeded energies that have made your acquaintance.

Know this! There is great responsibility when you begin to recycle energy. One must be anchored in the Ascended Heart Chakra and be present with the gift of true service. For many years chaotic energy has often been sent into the core of your planet. This practice must stop, as the time of releasing is upon you. Your planet has already begun its release, so anything you send into it will simply come back to you. It is time to release up to your brethren who are prepared and able to lovingly recycle this energy without harm. So let us teach you how to easily complete the process.

CREATING YOUR DIVINE CONTAINER

First, you must create the sacred container. Creating a container is simple. It must be of earthen material, and it must be placed upon the Earth. If one lives in an apartment without yard access, a small box of dirt would suffice to place the container on. The vessel must also be imprinted with the energy of the one who is creating it.

Once the container is created, you can complete the exercise in the presence of the container, or by simply visualizing the container you are aligned with.

While you can use this exercise at any time, it is optimal to set aside one time per week for formally releasing all of the energy which has been safely held in the container.

This is the TOSA world container. We placed our hands in colored paint and held the container, thereby literally imprinting it with our energy, and also added some symbols. You may decorate your container in any manner that brings you Joy!

(If you do not wish to create your own container, please use the TOSA world container pictured.)

THE DIVINE CONTAINER GALACTIC YOGIC PRACTICE

Begin by calling in a deep centering breath to the heart. Raise the right hand high above the head with the palm facing toward you. This is Posture A.

Posture A

Become aware of the energy that you are wishing to release. You may wish to call forth the energy of a stored hurt, or anger. You may also wish to release lack of clarity or any other condition of past or present experience. Once you call this energy forth, acknowledge it by declaring, "I Love You." This is an imperative step.

Acknowledging with love circumvents polarizing judgments, and enables the energy pattern to dissipate quickly.

163

Posture B

Posture C

Sweep the right hand down in front of all the traditional chakras (Posture B), and at the base chakra extend the hand outward (Posture C), and state: "To the container." If you are not in the physical presence of the container, visualize yourself releasing this energy into a container you are connected with [i.e., the TOSA container pictured on page 162].

Repeat this process as many times as needed to clear all that is present. There is no time limit. Know that you can always clear at any time during the day whenever you feel the need to discharge energy. Simply stop what you are doing, take in a deep breath, raise your right hand, acknowledge the energy by saying, "I love you," and send it to the container! [See Postures B and C.]

It is important to use the right hand. You must remember this. The right hand is the hand that releases energy. Do not use the left hand. This is VERY important! The left hand should be held with palm open, allowing you to receive Divine Love and to be in connection as you release with the right hand. It is also best to stand whenever you are able.

ENERGY AND EMOTIONS

When you accept an energy pattern that has come into your consciousness, how you integrate it can be disharmonious. Sometimes you energize through anger, sometimes through depression, sometimes through Joy, sometimes through Love, and sometimes by simply sitting and being—in meditation, for example.

All energization while you are in a physical form is directly attached to an emotional response. *This is how you can become trapped in the emotional body. It is the emotional body that is engaged as you meet and energize these patterns. It stores them according to how they are met.*

Recognize the power of being in the state of bliss and Joy. When you are in the state of bliss and Joy, every energy pattern that comes to you can only be met with bliss and Joy. No other patterning, such as emotional chaos, can attach to this energy, thereby drawing it into you.

When you are able to maintain the state of bliss and Joy, you are protected from anything that is sent your way as an interfering energy pattern because it cannot find a place to be energized, to latch on to, and stay. It will immediately transmute!

This is the freedom of staying in the Self-Ascended State and bringing the Ascended Chakra system into alignment. Let your heart be the root center! When you are no longer held captive by the issues of the traditional first, second, and third chakras, the energy patterns that once manifested through them have no power.

When your system is weakened by the energies attached to these three lower chakras, the fourth, fifth, sixth, and seventh chakras become influenced and tainted by the same unhealthy energy patterns. Those patterns will shift the true purpose of these upper chakras. Abundance, clarity, and true service all become challenging and elusive.

One must completely align with the heart as the root chakra of the Ascended State in order to maintain Peace, Love, and Joy. By doing so, you are impervious to all energy that is not aligned with your true service. It becomes quite simple. You see the energy. You are able to meet it. You make its acquaintance; however, you do not energize it. You are conscious of what you are energizing, and the need for all the exercises is not as compelling because there is nothing to clear.

Remember, when you make the acquaintance of any energy pattern, you do not have to energize it. Recognize that it is the emotional body that offers the attachment to all these patterns. This is the power of the emotional body. This is why the emotional body goes through so many fluctuations—because it is frequently and unconsciously aligning with different energetic patterns, sometimes many at once.

The Divine Container exercises serve to support bliss and Joy. Once you are in that space, you no longer have the need for the exercise. Know, however, that you will still need to do world clearing, and it is always good to double-check for a long time until you are sure about what is really inside of you. Remember, dearest ones, when you are sure you are complete, check again!

We have created a universal container that is now permanently placed at TOSA ranch. All are welcome to send energies to this container. Every Sunday evening at 7:00 p.m. Mountain Time, we release this container and call in all other containers for releasing. So have no fear—your container will always be able to receive as much energy as you wish to send to it. We encourage you to teach others this exercise and for you to know that you cannot ever "do it wrong." Your loving intent will always create the perfect environment!

SRI RAM KAA CONTINUES:

Over the years I have delighted as Kira and I have further trusted those of the Archangelic Realm and followed their guidance. Releasing certain foods, refining our home environment, and purifying on many levels have been required. She often wears shielded glasses to screen out artificial lighting. What some would call sacrifices we see as enhancements to deepen our Divine Connection.

One of the many gifts we both receive in conjunction with our commitment is the loving energy imprint of the Divine In-soulment. This is a healing energy, for we only In-soul those of the Archangelic and higher dimensions. Early one morning, my heart was moved to a new level when it was the Mother Mary who offered the following message:

> *Know. Know that I am with you. It is me, Mary.*
>
> *I have been requested by the Lord of Hosts to speak with you now with great love and concern. My message to the world has been, and is consistently, a return, a call to love, to greater love, to greater connection to the Oneness, to the Being, and to the gift of life. These terms, these words, have been misunderstood and misused many times.*
>
> *I love all.*
>
> *I love those who misunderstand, as much as I love those who misuse, as much as I love those who do understand.*
>
> *Unification is the goal.*
>
> *The unification of the Love of the One, and the return to the soul, the innocence.*
>
> *The return to the Truth, the return to the indisputable knowing of Love, the indisputable sharing of Love, the indisputable Oneness of the Power of the God of Hosts.*

Chapter Fourteen

COSMOLOGY AND REUNIFICATION

Before we go any farther here, take a moment and notice how you respond to this "new word." It is Tu'Laya. It is pronounced too-lay-ah. Allow yourself to say this word out loud and then simply close your eyes, take a deep breath, and say it again. Pay attention to what you experience, feel, or think! Just notice…avoid judgment…you are being prepared to lovingly break free of a paradigm.

Regardless of your personal standpoint on evolution, play along with us for just a moment here. Let's assume that humankind did not evolve from monkeys, though some scientists suggest that monkeys are our ancestors. Creating a vessel for our DNA was much more complicated and intentional than any model of Darwin's natural selection. Without debating the source of your biological jumpsuit, let us just remind you not to confuse "The You" with your vessel (body). "The You" is the one that occupies the vessel.

The Travelers began their journey into density on a world thought to be Leumeria. In fact it was named Tu'Laya, and this extraordinary adventure existed in another dimension. The next experience in density was on a world called Atlantis. The Earth is the third and final expression of spirit into matter. This form of density experience is now completing itself, hence the reunification energies that culminate in 2012, and indeed have already begun.

In the following discourse Archangel Zadkiel offers a brief cosmology.

ARCHANGEL ZADKIEL: *Dearest children, it is indeed the time of the Tu'Layan expansion and the reintegration of all Atlantean energy. Do you understand what this means? It means a lot, oh boy! So we will take it in little pieces for you.*

In this world now many talk about Mu...you know Mu? They talk about Mu, they talk about Leumeria, and they talk about Atlantis, and they all talk about them in many different ways. Everyone has great fantasy stories, do they not? They are so much fun!

Yes, embrace every story; they are all perfection! They are all fun! For indeed in each individual story, in each individual expression, is the perfection of that which in your cellular DNA is wanting to reconnect and remember. So every story is correct, every single one.

Each must have their experience. Each must have their memory. Each must have their knowing. All we wish to offer you in this moment now is a cosmology and an understanding of how these energies have come forth. Take them in and integrate them. How you move forward is your own resolution. It is your time for complete resolution of everything. Resolve all that within yourself feels unresolved.

In this time of true resolution and culmination, call back all that you are into the wholeness that you deserve to be. You are whole. If you are holding onto old hurts, ask yourself who are you holding onto them for? Who do they serve? Ask yourself this question. If you wish to be in pain, go for it, do it well! And if you wish to be hurt, go for it, hurt well.

When you have said, "been there, done that," you can let it go just as quickly. It is indeed your culminating time and you must understand that many will culminate in pain as many will culminate in Joy. It is OK. How do you choose to bring forth your culmination?

LET US TALK ABOUT COSMOLOGY

When you began expansion as the Travelers, you came forth from Light with great Love and great Joy. You have great expansionary ability, and your first expression in subtle density was in the time that many have referred to as the Leumerian experience. This was before the seeding on this planet and the experience that many have called Mu. You must understand, dearest children, that all of the experiences that all understand and that all have brought forth did all exist. There are none that did not exist. There is no right or wrong here. There is the Allness.

It is your time to recognize the Allness within. From within, the Truth emerges from your own DNA. Within your own cellular structure there cannot be doubt, there cannot be words, there cannot be confusion, because you are resonating from a stream of conscious Truth.

Conscious Truth cannot be given to you. You do not receive it from somebody else.

YOU CALL IT FORTH FROM WITHIN

In your conscious Truth you recognize that you have expanded for eons. Let go of your concept of what time is. If you go into the concept of what time is for you, it will become most frustrating. Your brain will blow up, literally, and sometimes that is not such a bad thing, no? If you wish to blow up your brain, go for it! Allow yourself to expand into the subtle densities of the Tu'Layan experience in the subtle realms, from which all pieces, all pieces of the spark of Divinity came forth, and all expressions were made available. You were brilliant and glorious and light-filled, as you are now. You experienced many different realms, many different capacities, and made many choices. As you made your choices, these realms have come forward. As you expanded into ever greater forms of density, you brought forth the first experience of Atlantis.

In the first experience of Atlantis, much was learned and much was understood. Your multidimensional capacity was extremely, as you would say, right on. It was most full. And in the fullness of your multidimensional experience and in the understanding of how all elements work together, in the connection of the streams of Light and the service of Love, you came forth again to this planet now. There had indeed been preparations made long before your coming to this planet. Many preparations! And in those preparations you again experienced your Leumerian life from the perspective of Earth. You experienced Atlantis again from the experience of Earth, as you are experiencing the now.

It is important to review what has been shared regarding cosmology:

1. Our first experience as the Travelers was one of subtle density. It was not the physical form we are currently familiar with; however, it was a form of density when compared to existence as Pure Light.

2. This first experience was in Tu'Laya, which many call Leumeria, and it existed in the 25th dimension. (There WAS a Leumeria on Earth; however, it was a seeding of this original existence.)

3. The next experience in density was Atlantis, a fifth-dimensional experience, which was located on Mars. (As with Leumeria, there WAS an Atlantis on Earth, only it occurred much later as a seeding of the original Mars expression, and is part of the Earth experience.)

4. Both of these prior expressions were not on Earth; however, energies from both of these expressions were later seeded on Earth in preparation for this third expansion through the experience of density, which has had many cycles.

ARCHANGEL ZADKIEL: *We wish for a moment to stop the cosmology lesson, and talk about Ancient Egypt. For many of you, it was during the early dynasties of what you call Ancient Egypt, that many of you here were indeed in pharaoh form, in queen form, in temple-service form. You were in many forms—many, many, many!*

Through those forms, you called back and understood this cosmology fully. You were in complete recognition of all of this. This is not new information for you; it is simply recognition of a cellular memory. In those times, in those expressions, it was then that many different markers were placed into this planet, for this time, now.

You are revealing the markers. Your presence is revealing the markers. You right now are unwrapping the truth of your being-ness. You are understanding where your alignments are. You are bringing forth your energies. Some say, "Oh, Leumeria! Oh my goodness! I can tell you days, dates, times, who I was with, what I did, etc." Good! Bring it forward! "Oh, Atlantis! I know what I did." Good! Bring it forward! "Oh, Egypt! I know what I did." Good! Bring it forward! **It is important now to recognize that you cannot be wrong in your own recognition of your truth of these experiences.** *Only you can doubt yourself, and doubt is the only energy that will separate you from this truth.*

It is important now to reintegrate all experiences during this time without becoming preoccupied with them! Preoccupation will create separation. Your culmination, this time of coming forward, is to remember. To re-member yourself! **You must remember yourself without doubt.** *Some may question your recollections and claim you are crazy. You know who you were; you know what you are through your being-ness!*

The knowing of who you are, the truth of your being-ness now—this is the gift that you must call forth during this time of connection. It is the year of bringing all of these pieces of energy back into one, into the you that you are now. How do you wish to energize your body? Whom do you wish to align with? What energies feel good for you? What words feel right for you? What understandings do you want to bring forward? You see, dearest children, we have been asking you to make your decision. Are you ready to embrace fifth- dimensional energies, or are you ready to stay in the third dimension? Which one do you choose to be in?

You are at the time in which fullness, your birthright, is upon you. What do you choose to be full of? Oh, that is a loaded question! [audience laughter] Many around you will be "full of," we assure you! So it is good to be full of you, full of your presence, full of your knowing, and full of your remembrance. Be filled with the trust of the truth of your being. In the trust of the truth of your being, all unfolds, and all unfolds effortlessly.

Are you moving with the flow? Is the flow around you? Where are you, and where do you wish to go?

Dearest ones, it is a time of great culmination. Each of you has the star within your forehead that you call forth as a means of being able to activate, understand, and be present with. All you need do is take your energy to this star. All you need do is trust what is revealed in front of you. Yes, this is the time of great alignments.

Many, many, many beings of the four soul groups will be coming back into their pure groups, meaning that you will find the wholeness of your own soul energy. The soul groups that have emerged on this planet have been many times split and separated and moved forward. You are at the time now when they are all coming back into reunification in many different ways. Hold open your portal of reunification.

Understand that in the time of cosmology, there is no right and wrong. There is the enfoldment. You are folding time upon yourself. Your days are already occurring with much more rapidity than they have before. You say, "Oh my goodness, so much to do, so little time, so little time, so much to do." How does that work? Letting go of time! We implore you again to let go of time.

Be in the Divine flow of this time. As you are in the Divine flow of this time, much is expanding around you. How do you wish it to manifest? Get very, very, very clear. Your manifestation abilities are beyond anything you can understand on this level. What do you really want? You must come forward within your own heart. If your head wishes to be in charge, then give it a good ride. Yes, get on that pony. [much laughter]

In your heart you understand all that is expanding now. In your heart you are able to manifest with ever greater understanding. Understand yourself first. We are grateful you are here. In your energies, in your presence, in your recognition, in your coming forth, in your ability to hold consciousness of who you are and what you are manifesting, you give others permission to do the same.

Dearest ones, you are pioneers. You must understand that! You are the Travelers. You have pioneered. You have done this all before, and each time it is experienced anew. We honor you! Think for a moment: you are sitting in a country (USA) where many came across in little covered wagons. Do you think they had padded seats? [audience laughter] No cruise control!

My goodness, there was no highway—they made the highway. Know that you are the highway, and you are making it every moment of every day. Do you recognize how amazing you are? Do you understand now your creative abilities? You are amazing creators and you have done this all before.

In this time of great energetic culmination, you are such a short time away from a rapid and quantum shift in how this planet will vibrate. Where will you be? Where would you like to be? It is very easy, dearest ones, to stay in density, is it not? It is very simple. You say, "Oh, but sometimes it can be downright painful—bills to pay, things to do, people to talk to." OK, even so, it's easy; you know how to do it. You know that thrill, as you have done it, been there, many times.

Is it not easy to be in fifth-dimensional energies now? Yes, it is. It is just simple because you have been there, done that. You do know it. All you need do is release the concept that it must look like this in every way. In many ways there are many similarities; in many ways you are gifted with great comfort, great comfort! Do not despair! When you despair, you offer yourself an emotional barrier to fifth-dimensional entry.

Keep your eyes on the Divine at all times, dearest ones. Go up into the Star Consciousness that you have accepted and look for the Divine within. Radiate your Divine Energy to the Divine around you. Greet each other, Divine to Divine. If you keep your eyes on the Divine at all times, no matter what shifts in front of you, you are with the Divine Energy. Your Divine Energy is present within. It is already culminating. How do you wish it to express?

Each is aligning in the dimensional realms where they are of greatest service now. All are offering themselves that opportunity. The only surprise will be those in density who are surprised! It is important for you to recognize that many shifts are in great preparation now. It is important to recognize that your bodies have carried you far and are ready to carry you farther.

Many, many, many, many of you have transmuted not only your own energies, but energies for many others. Know this! In transmutation of these energies, your bodies have indeed felt this transmutation. Your bodies know what you are up to. They know even when the mind doesn't.

Many may have frustration with their bodies. It is important to recognize that body frustration is nothing more than a call to Density Consciousness. Allow yourself the opportunity to simply love the body, appreciate it, honor it, stay present with it. If it needs a few extra pounds, oh well, have fun. If it needs a few less pounds, oh well, have fun. Be present! Let it be! If it calls you from knees, hips, elbows, or joints, and says, "Hey, what are you doing?" say, "I am loving you," and offer love back.

You must be in Divine Connection with the body now—you must be! The body is already aligning with energies that your mind may not wish to understand.

QUESTION: Where was Atlantis and where was Leumeria?

Oh, good question. However, it is a twofold question, is it not? Are you asking for here, this Earth, or are you asking prior to here?

QUESTION: Prior to here.

Of course you are! The Leumerian, or Tu'Layan, which is the proper name, was the first subtle-density expression of Light as Travelers. Tu'Laya existed in a galaxy that is not recognizable from this realm right here. It is, however, a subtle galaxy that has expressions of density that exist in the 25th dimension. In the 25th dimension, you brought forth great recognition of many sparks of density.

It was in the Tu'Layan expression and the Tu'Layan expansion that you called forth the opportunity to express in density ever more. Coming forth into this realm that you are in now, into this galaxy now, there were what you call planets that were identified for you to be present on.

The expression of Atlantis existed very close to here, dear one. It existed on a planet that you now know as Mars. On Mars, the Atlantean expression was fully realized and, dearest child, your scientists now already have this evidence. They are already aware of this civilization energy.

In the time of Atlantis when you knew that it was time to leave, you were on Mars as part of the seeding of this planet, Earth, to further prepare the crystalline grids in this planet, grids that are realigning now. The crystalline grid realignments that are coming forward are setting forth numerous vibrational shifts.

It was in the time of the Egyptian ancient dynasties that those of you who seeded from these other galaxies came forth with your own energies. You looked very different. In that time, you brought forth and set in motion all of the necessary energies that are coming back right now.

QUESTION: Is everybody on the planet now here via Atlantis, or is there a big group of people from Atlantis?

This is a good question! This is a cosmology question. You must recognize that, on this planet now, the majority of the people are from the four soul groups. This planet is now also host to many from other realms. The majority that are on this planet now did have an Atlantean experience; however, not all had that experience in form, as you would call it. Some were simply energies that were present at that time. Yes, your planet is rich with many, many different expressions. They are all here now as part of the time of culmination. That is why this time it is imperative for you to get very crystal clear on knowing your gifts, your truths, and your being-ness.

Understanding cosmology is similar to understanding your past lives. It offers you a context for your expression in the now. It also helps you understand the extent to which you have traveled from Source, and the significance of the reunion. It truly is a time of galactic Joy, for the Travelers are coming home! Many blessings!

As the home of Atlantis, Mars was once a planet of crystalline clear waters, great mountains, temples, and vast technologies. It is little wonder that our government is interested in Mars, for many secrets are buried beneath the surface of this planet.

We include this photo of Mars as a reminder, both of a former homeland and of the destruction that can occur as technology advances while Divine Connectivity is displaced. Our hearts have learned the lessons of Atlantis. This is why so many are dedicated to honoring the Earth. We have agreed to culminate in a gentler fashion this time around!

UNDERSTANDING REFRACTION

The game, so to speak, since the time of creation, was to refract the One Light into many pieces and then watch those conscious pieces of Light refract themselves even further, over and over. This offered great Joy to Source. Each refraction takes what was whole and breaks it into pieces. Yet, like a hologram, each piece is complete and contains Soul. Over the millennia, there can be billions (zillions!) of pieces created! This refraction into diversity includes the outer world as well as our inner world of beliefs and thoughts. This is the expression of Light into Allness. Wow…what an amazing universe of creation! Allness is everything…every possible point of view…every possible loving act and every possible evil act. It is ALL available, and by necessity it is all expressed. This mind-boggling expansion can not be held by the Earth brain…only the mind of God can find the Joy of such expansive diversity and infinite creation.

The imperative for the "children of God," the Light, was to "go forth and multiply." Light is constantly moving forward, expanding and refracting. The imperative to expand has resulted in Light taking every imaginable expression. From the standpoint of the Creator Source, all of this is Good, for it is all Self-expression.

Consider for a moment that you are a powerful Being of Light, a child of God. There is nothing in the universe that can kill you. Yes, you could lose your body (which is a temporary creation, analogous to an overcoat that can be thrown away and then re-created). You can experience pain and loss. These are momentary truths. However, the You that you essentially are is immortal, even if you fear otherwise. Thus, the sense of identity you hold is a refraction, a distortion of the Immortal Truth, and is applicable only to this lifetime. Even if you believe in and are fully committed to this refracted mortal identity, this mortal personality, you still won't die. You will simply invent another expression for your essential energy…a new refraction after the current one is dropped.

While our intent is not to challenge your mind with new beliefs, we are inviting your mind to loosen its grip on perceived reality. Recognize that the grip you may presently have, whatever belief structure you trust, is limited. Beliefs too are choices. They are refractions, a subset, incomplete versions of something else. Beliefs serve to stabilize your mind and your emotions, and in that stability, in that "nailing down" of "facts," your soul is also nailed down, and growth is resisted.

As we enter this time of rapid transformation you may feel as if you are losing your mind. This is a good sign; it means you are expanding through the old structures and coming to a new, more unified structure. The zillions of refractions, like many small puzzle pieces, are now being reunified. As we cycle toward Oneness we must integrate the Allness, the infinite expressions of creation. That's a big job! Each of us will integrate our soul's journey as we return home.

THE RETURN TO ONENESS HAPPENS THROUGH ALL OF US

Many of the ancients knew that a time of reunification was coming. The Mayans were taught that all cycles culminate, and each cycle incorporates the wisdom of the prior time. They know that our Light (our true essence) is coming forward now. This cosmic wisdom was also woven into the consciousness of the Hopi, the Dogon, the Hindu, and many other cultures. The prophecies of destruction in the coming times expand upon the instability that we must experience as we change. Institutions created from lower levels of consciousness will have to change. The fact that greater Light is seeking to emerge brings new Unity and Love to our shared world. This is a great Joy. We are headed toward a new Unity—a truth that was also hidden and distorted by those who believed you should not know.

There are forces in the universe that do not want you to reunify. These energies are intelligent and actively interfering with the reunification process. Yet, they are not to be feared. The third dimension is a realm of duality. Its very nature is a split away from Oneness in order to explore polarity. Everything created and birthed into this dimension has an essential falsehood woven into its very core. That falsehood is duality, which is seeming separateness from the Divine. Thus, the refraction from Oneness into individualization is woven into third-dimensional beliefs. There are some who are so committed to these beliefs and energies that they will actively try to fight Unity.

Remember, a belief pattern defines your reality. So, if you believe that the Earth is flat, then any evidence to the contrary is discarded. This is why "true believers" burn books—they have no tolerance or understanding for a contrary point of view. Whether their commitment to their faith is fear-driven or inspired, matters not. The fact is, their commitment creates a hierarchy that devalues other perspectives and perpetuates the energy of polarity. As long as polarity is energized, those at the top of the food chain, so to speak, stay fat and happy.

This is one of the reasons the Illuminati,[56] and those who are aligned with them, do not want you to wake up. They keep and savor the spoils of power and control over third-dimensional reality as long as there are other players in the game. So the Illuminati and those who have aligned with their values and beliefs really want the status quo to continue. If you decide to Self-Ascend and anchor in another dimension to express your Light, then their game board gets darker.

The Illuminati are no more evil than you or I. They are simply expressing their own limiting beliefs and density addiction through this dimensional experience. They have full access to the shadow side of mankind's consciousness and thus can whip up some fairly nasty situations on the game board. That is, pestilence, disease, and war are all selections on their creation pallet. However, they cannot create these effects without your help. Your consciousness, your energy, helps the negative take form in our world.

Quantum physics has taught us that the material world will reflect our consciousness back to us. The depth and significance of this is so mind-boggling that most people do not wrap around the notion that they themselves are creating the polarity. Mankind is conditioned to believe in a "power" "out there" that is pulling the strings. This concept prevents us from recognizing that we *are* that power. As the Hopi have said, "We are the ones we have been waiting for." Are you ready to accept your power?

Like children growing through developmental stages, mankind must suffer the evolutionary growing pains and sorrow attendant upon emotional growth, and find the Joy of true power. Joy is an expansive energy. It opens us to possibilities and invites creativity and delight. Yet, following our Joy—"or bliss," as Joseph Campbell so brilliantly taught—is hard, for it means we must set aside the delusions of child-hood and adolescence and be responsible. This means cultivating our sense of Joy. Joy is feedback from the soul. Following your soul's Joy requires the commitment of the density body. Your ego must trust the soul or it will sabotage your authentic Joy.

Self-Ascension is the process of redefining your sense of identity apart from the body, from the ego, and from any role or career identity, while simply knowing that you are the core essence of consciousness. You, and I, and all your friends and seeming enemies, are the "I AM that I AM." This can happen in an instant, yet it usually takes years of evolutionary steps that culminate in that instant.

Many people walk this planet claiming that they know the truth of who they are, yet those same people get ill, experience fear, and lack the Self-trust. They are unable to live in true alignment with their soul. There is a stage in awakening in which we know what to do, but we have not yet done it. This is when we have all the right words and yet still in many matters conform to the "norms" of the group. This is quite normal...and must be grown through. Recognition of this stage is actu-ally cause for celebration.

If you truly know your soul, then you will never experience separation from God. If you truly trust your soul, then you love yourself always, in all-ways. The soul is the essence of unconditional love and it resides right within and as you. You are that! For countless millennia, we have cultivated a multitude of differentiated expressions and have lost sight of the Oneness. Being hypnotized into believing we are separate from the Divine means that our creations, our refractions, seem to take us ever farther from Oneness.

MORE ABOUT THE ILLUMINATI

The Illuminati are the topic of controversy and fear in those who speak of them. Despite their name, the Illuminati are no more or less illuminated than anyone else. They are beings just like you and I. The one advantage they have is that, for the most part, when they incarnate into bodies they stay connected to their brethren who are not in body. This means that the nonphysical Illuminati can guide or influence one who is in body. As the nonphysical realm is the fourth dimension or astral realm, there is more freedom of expression there. The fourth dimension is a realm of dreams, ghosts, and instant manifestation of thought forms. There is no gross physical form and there is no sense of time. The astral entities are completely preoccupied by the world of form.

Resident in the astral dimension, the Illuminati find great nourishment and vicarious pleasure in dominating the emotions of the physically embodied. They literally feed on the free-floating fear and violence. It is like food to them. They also want to preserve a sense of power by being able to provoke the players on the game board into patterns of servitude and fear. Being a slave to money, being a slave to power, being an addict or a warrior, all serve to stimulate ever more excitement, fear, and attachment to the game board. These energies serve the Illuminati.

All the lessons of the game board also serve you. You are the one developing discernment. You are the one who seeks to learn more about love and the experience of pain. You are the one who seeks to discern the difference between true power and false power. You are the one who needs to learn that force does not cultivate true alignment. Many lessons. Many lifetimes.

When is enough, enough? When you decide that you are complete.

Chapter Fifteen

DOES EVERYONE
HAVE A SOUL MATE?

Completion is the call to wholeness. This desire expresses itself in many ways upon our planet. With ever greater passion and rising complexity, the craving for soul connection has rapidly increased on all levels. In our travels around this amazing planet, at every event we appear at, inevitably we are asked: "How can I find my soul mate, and how can I have a relationship like yours?"

Regardless of the Quantum Leap approaching us, or our hunger to participate in the universe, it is this basic yearning that still propels the actions of most. The sincerity of this yearning for true union—beyond sex, familial obligation, or worldly success—cannot be denied. And from this springs the obvious question: Why are we preoccupied with union?

Know that collectively, we have already entered into a new relationship with ourselves, with each other, and with the universe. The four primary soul groups are presently in the process of reunification in final preparation for the leap in consciousness that is upon us, now.

Many are being called to new interactions with those they love, especially since the karmic release at the millennium. Recognize that Partnership is the energy of the Quantum Leap, not relationship. Relationships are now failing and will continue to fail as part and parcel of the energy that is clinging to Density Consciousness.

Relationship = Me in relation to You
Partnership = Us

Partnership must be accepted as the new paradigm for couples. While this may not seem new to you in concept, go beyond your physical mind and enter the Realm of Ascension Awareness. We know from the Pyramid of Spiritual Awakening that the levels of Density Consciousness and Spiritual Activism embody, to some extent, both judgment and a "me vs. you" orientation. They are the perfect environment in which the relationship model to flourish.

Yet, if you have become aware of your own energetic realignment in relation to the universal flow, chances are you have also undergone serious relationship failure at one time or another. Untold numbers of couples who have tolerated lukewarm complacency for years are rapidly separating, due to the need for one or both to realign with vibrationally compatible partners. Many more are simply refusing to enter into relationship at all, knowing that interactions with any who are not energetically aligned would be futile.

FROM SACRED UNION: THE JOURNEY HOME

"What most people refer to as a Soul Mate is actually a Karmic Mate."

This relationship is characterized by a magnetic attraction and perhaps a sense of resolution. The Sacred Union, on the other hand, is characterized by a sense of completion. Because it has never happened before, the feelings and perceptions attendant upon the Sacred Union may be unlike anything you have ever experienced."[57]

Prior to the millennium, we often fell in love because of the inner excitement of having found someone for karmic resolution. The magnetism of the karmic imperative brought us together. In recent years, with the release of karma, people are being called to find their true energetic counterparts. These partnerships bring people of the same soul groups together for their mutual expansion and reunion in consciousness.

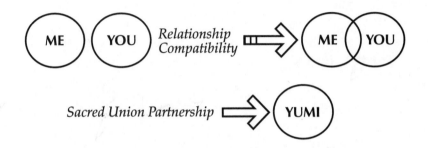

The above diagram shows the past paradigm of me and you coming together in relationship, still as a me and a you. In Sacred Union, the me and the you completely merge, becoming the Yumi[58] soul. It's not that the you or the me is lost; rather, there are neither secrets nor energetic hold-backs. The Union is complete.

When we understand the difference between a karmic-mate relationship and a Sacred Union Partnership, the impact becomes clear. With the release of karmic obligation, the opportunity to claim self-responsibility as a conscious co-creator is upon us now. Whether mindfully conscious of this choice or not, at a cellular level all beings are experiencing this call to completion.

Simply put, the relationship of the self is now seeking partnership with the universe. Breaking free of the chaotic energy stream of density frees you to experience partnership in all-ways! Conversely, aligning with the chaotic density offers a relationship playground on which one experiences repetitive patterns, repeatedly deriving lessons from those patterns until a new choice is made.

"In the world of duality, everything is a relationship. In the world of Oneness, everything is love."[59]

Understanding soul groups requires more than a chapter, and indeed warrants full attention as its own book. Know in this moment that you can recognize your own partnership with the universe at any time.

When Archangel Zadkiel first offered information to us about the four soul groups on the planet, the differences between relationship and partnership became clear. It also expanded our understanding of ourselves, and why we are all seeking reunification at this time.

THE FOUR TYPES OF SOUL GROUPS ARE:

1. **Union:** Souls that were birthed as one. They were separated at the end of the density experience of Atlantis—literally split in half. They are seeking to reunify with their other soul-half. These souls seek deep Union with one who is carrying the same energy signature, literally their "other half." They may have had many marriages in their search for this Union. Often, they have held a lifelong remembrance of another "half." Most union souls will never give up on partnership, despite many perceived relationship failures.

2. **Omni:** Souls that have always remained as one experience of light throughout all density experiences. They are complete without a partner, being in fullness with the Divine always, although they may not be aware of this connection until later in life. Often this group tries to enter into relationships only to find them temporary. Until self-realized, they can be perceived as non-caring, quick to end relationships, or detached and leery of commitment. They are simply whole within themselves. They usually find peace through quiet communion with the Divine (or themselves, until fully realized). Omni souls make ideal nuns or monks.

3. **Dual:** Souls birthed as one complete soul, yet have another Divine counterpart (similar to twins). Different from the Union soul, they are whole as individuals yet find greater Divine Communion with their counterpart. Often confused with the Union soul, Dual souls

are looking for their "cosmic twin" who, when found, may even look physically alike. However, they can find earthly fulfillment without their counterpart, as may the Omni. Dual souls are in fact complete within themselves. They can also expand their recognition of consciousness in Sacred Partnership with their twin, similar to the dynamics of the Union soul.

Dual souls

4. **Multi-expressional:** Souls that have always embodied many expressions of light, and seek to incorporate all expressions. Birthed as one soul, they have the capacity to express in many ways, and often have done this throughout the universe. Multi-expressional souls have a built-in desire to integrate all of their experiences with as many as possible. It is their way of bringing all experiences back to the Divine. This group often embraces polyamory[60] and may find it challenging to stay in a committed relationship for very long. They love to exchange energy, and are best suited to be in partnership with one another, or with a fully realized Omni.

As you review these soul groups, remember that you are viewing them from the standpoint of reverse engineering. These four groups were birthed as The Travelers. Throughout our experiences of density, they have further refined themselves, split again and again, and lost their distinctions in the constructs of this planet.

In modern times, many people have yearned for a soul mate, and many have felt frustrated. As you welcome the discernment regarding the four soul groups, it will become easier to understand why some relationships never quite "fit," even though the people involved had similar values and interests.

We are beyond the time when fitting together at the personality level is enough. Yearning for true energetic alignment and deep congruence, the soul groups are coming back together and recreating the pure stream of energy. Many are finding themselves called into new partnerships as a result of this yearning for alignment.

These expressions of light form the original intent of the Travelers to enrich the experience of expansion through adventures in density. Scanning the four groups, you are most likely looking for yourself. You are in there! Recognizing your own soul energy can help you understand your particular experiences in relationship and partnership. A deep inner peace is found through reunion with one's true soul group. Years of event-responses, especially in areas of relationship and partnership, suddenly make sense. Actions and ways of being that may have been shrouded by societal judgment are understood, thereby relaxing self-judgment and creating the spaciousness that is self-love.

Many ask: "Does it matter what soul group my partner comes from?" This is a valuable question, and the answer is yes and no. The response depends largely upon the soul group and emotional maturity of the questioner. A basic compatibility chart is included below; however, anyone can transcend density energy and be complete with another in the fifth dimension. Remember, we are all one. Soul groups emerged as original creations, expressing as sparks of light. The chart will guide you in finding the "ah-ha" moment for yourself, past relationships, and perhaps your perfect partnership.

SOUL GROUP	CHARACTERISTICS	BEST WITH
Union	Seek reunification Many relationships "Knowing" of another	Union
Omni	Seek to not feel alone Perceived as distant Find peace with God	Omni Multi-expressional
Dual	Seek Themselves Complete alone Better in Partnership	Dual Union
Mulit-expressional	Seek many experiences Enjoy multiple partners Important to integrate	Multi-expressional Omni

ARCHANGEL ZADKIEL: *All of these soul groups are returning to their wholeness with Source now. They are reunifying back into pure soul-group expression.*

QUESTION: Please talk about Sacred Union. It feels like the energy on the planet now is balancing the male and female at a higher frequency. Many people are not able to be in it. I just met my twin flame and he couldn't hold it, so we separated. It feels like the work now is to prepare people to shift into that energy. Could you say something about what it is?

This is very much part of the mission of Self-Ascension—to offer the gift of Sacred Union. Now what is Sacred Union? Sacred Union begins with the understanding, the deep understanding, of the wholeness of the self. This is why, as you say, many are unable to hold the energy. Many come together and can't seem to be there. Yes, in the time of escalation there are many who are coming into Sacred Union. Some are coming into Sacred Union in partnership, and others are coming into Sacred Union in alignment. Some are coming into Sacred Union with the truth of those they are meant to be with.

There are many forms of Sacred Union. It is all about the balancing, not so much of the man/woman. It is a balancing of the masculine/feminine energies. This is an important distinction. It is energy balancing. It does not matter, man—man, woman—woman; this does not matter. What matters is the balance of the energies.

As these energies start balancing, egos begin flaring! Egos enjoy imbalance and flourish in imbalance. This is how they gain more control. As one comes into union of the wholeness of the self, the first thing that happens as the balancing energy enters is the flaring of the ego. This is especially noticeable when one is in the presence of their beloved partner. This will do it quickly!

This is important to understand, especially if one has taken in the wholeness of Truth. If one has said, "Yes! I understand the gift of being in wholeness," then the sacred partner can mirror that wholeness. When the ego comes up, it is the opportunity to clear, move forward, and come into union.

Also know that when one is in partnership but cannot hold space at that time, each still has the opportunity to be in Sacred Union with the truth of their own wholeness. There is always a gift, dear one. As we move into Sacred Union, it is directly tied to our ability to be in Self-Ascension.

Ascend back to the truth of who you are, live in that state, and keep your eyes on the Divine. Open up the heart chakra as the root chakra, and move through the four steps of Self-Ascension.[61]

THE FOUR STEPS OF SELF-ASCENSION

Step One: *Be in union. This is often misunderstood. To be in union is about being in union with you. It is not about partnership. You must first be in union with your wholeness, understanding the truth of who you are.*

Step Two: *Release judgment. You judge constantly here because you are in a judgmental, dualistic world! As you release the judgment, you move forward. You are able to hold the space of union and not bring judgment into any partnership.*

Step Three: *Unconditional Love. This begins with the self. Unconditional Love is a practice, is it not?*

Step Four: *Surrender. Through all relationships, you are given the opportunity to surrender, are you not? When you fully surrender all to the Divine, the Divine can then offer you the abundance you seek in all aspects of the expression of light that you are.*

Unlock your own Divine power. Keep your eyes focused straight ahead. Do not look side to side. Give yourself the gift of training. Gift yourself often, because you deserve it! It is a time of Joy. It is a time of re-union. It is a time of communion. It is a time of Divine Connection. Many blessings! We love you dearly! Many blessings!

WHAT ABOUT SOUL CONTRACTS?

This powerful question was addressed by a group we call the Benevolent Ones. These Divine Beings are pure energy and hold open a portal of light directly from the Archangels to the Elohim. The Benevolent Ones offer profound clarity and love with their dispensations, and often require reading and rereading in order to fully appreciate the energy and wisdom in their communications. Here is their response to the question regarding soul contracts:

This question is a request for discernment. You are asking to find a filter of discernment, for this is not a question of selfish action. It is important to understand that many have endured great pains through their multiple experiences of density to be able to fulfill the contractual understanding that leads to an agreement.

Presently on your planet, there is much languaging, and many misunderstandings with respect to the perception of contracts. Many declare that they have a contract for this or for that, or with this one or that one. This word "contract" is not of a light language; it is a word of density.

A contract implies an agreement that must be explicitly spelled out, agreed to, and signed. The existence of a contract also implies ramifications according to its interpretation. All of these concepts are born in density, are they not? Even the word "contract" comes from a density misunderstanding of soul alignment.

We very carefully choose our words because there are so few to choose from and because they are indeed most limiting. Yet, your words are precious and they are necessary at this time to offer greater expansion. Without words, there would be the egoic filter within applied to an interpretation of an energy transmission offered. Would this not lead to ever more confusion and misunderstanding?

So, through these words, we offer you expansionary and infinite wisdom into the realm of energetic receptivity. That is the truth of what this realm has manifested, not a principle and belief system known as a contract.

It is most important to recognize that each being of expansion, each spark of Divine Light, has only one agreement—to expand. The word "agreement" limits understanding of the expansion. It is indeed an energetic alignment that propels energy. When energy meets resistance, it will find a way to move around or through the resistance. It can do this by expanding and encompassing the resistance into it, to swallow it, as you would say.

Visualize a little stream of light coming up to a square wall. As the light meets the wall, the stream expands to become a circle that is larger than the square. The square then becomes part of the circle and the stream keeps moving. This is very much the principle of energy expansion.

Energy expands when it meets challenges that ask it to shift. It does not alter the universal principle of expansion; it simply asks it to become ever more available.

We mention this to offer understanding of the misinterpretation of the energetic principles that have become the basis and foundation of expansion while you are in density. It is through the collusion of many energies on this planet with energies not of this planet that the perceived need for a contract comes about.

As you have expanded through Tu'Laya to Atlantis to this expression now, the concept of ever-expanding density along with the contractual concept has been refined. It was born and then expanded. You must understand that because you are coming back into full alignment, the circle has indeed swallowed the square.

It is as if you see a snake eat a rat. The neck of the snake gets very big at first and eventually digests the rat lower down. The square is being minimized now, and the stream will continue unaffected, however more enhanced.

Imagine your contract concept is the square, and there have been many eons of expansion to finally encompass that which has tried to resist. This is the only example we can offer you that can begin to conceptualize the truth of this energy pattern.

You have asked us how this process can be easier for the body. This experience of the body is your own creation. We offer information without interpretation so that there is no misinterpretation. The expression of density that all are living now is dissolving into the limitlessness. As you begin dissolving into limitlessness, many dimensions become present at once. Many expressions of your own being-ness are available at once.

As you dissolve, the egoic filters are no longer necessary, and initially what you would consider to be an etheric dampener becomes removed, thereby startling the body. There is also misinterpretation of what is seen, what is heard, and yes, what is known.

Your bodies of flesh are being trained, prepared, and enhanced, so that they may be more readily accepting of their own limitations. The flesh body accepts no limitation as it is ruled by the mind. The mind body creates the illusion, and the etheric body seeks only to protect. You must recognize that as you are allowing the free-floating atoms and molecules of limitlessness to bind with the molecules of flesh, together they can move.

The body of flesh must take in and realign with the molecules of limitlessness. As you do this more, you will have more experiences. All that you feel within the physical realm is physical resistance that is not connected to the mind, that is not connected with the spirit. You cannot judge it, and you cannot eliminate it through your own desire to understand. It is without mind. It simply is.

In your desire to reduce, eliminate, and understand, there is actually energy given to this energy of discomfort. It is unnecessary to give it energy. It is more important for you to simply love without having to consciously send love. What we mean is that if you must stop and pay attention to a discomfort, then you have still not integrated enough love into the body. The only practice you need then is to practice allowing love to be the body.

This can be very confusing because in the realm of density, love is so misunderstood. The love that we offer you is an energetic vibration that resonates with harmonic balance and sustains universal limitlessness through harmony. This love is already present. It is through the declaration of "I AM" that one calls forth this understanding, and it is also through movement, recognition, and breathing.

Give the love through action, not through your words. Feel it pulsing through you, and you will know its sustenance; in its sustenance there is great action. Simply offer what is, so that each may call forth their own understanding. You are spending greater time in greater realms; limitlessness is not a task; it simply is.

It is beneficial in times of fear to be in close proximity with your loved ones. Offer loving eye contact without judgment. Great energy simply offered through eye contact offers Divine reassurance. This reassurance must come from the understanding of Truth. It could be as simple as send-

ing the message, "We are in a moment of limitlessness. We are in a moment of remembrance. Your body knows this. Our bodies are safe."

This should not be a job. Delight in the conscious knowing. It is only the energy of habitual density that wishes to make you feel you must prepare to delight. Delight is already here. The limitlessness is you, around you, everything, all.

We come to you in joyous recognition as the patterns of alignment are moving. There is no timeline except the one you set for yourself. There is patience, tolerance, and there is also the forcing of energy. You cannot force your energy to be patient, nor can you tolerate the intolerable. Allow yourself to have your patience be present, and delight. From that, all you see is already done. There is nothing you need know for all is known. Release the concept of the contract so that you may be free to embrace energetic alignment.[62]

This teaching from the Benevolent Ones is pure, concise, and rooted in galactic truth. It takes some practice for the density brain to relax its expectations and allow the message to be fully understood.

This discourse offers more depth than simply exploring the topic of contracts. In order to understand that our souls seek alignments, it is useful to understand how we separated and how we are realigning. We encourage you to reread this sharing, and have included it to offer your consciousness an ever greater level of expansion and recognition.

EMPOWERING THE ANGEL WITHIN: NOURISHING SOUL CONSCIOUSNESS

To our great delight, over 75% of the population believes in Angels, a powerful statistic and one with solid foundation. Even among those who do not believe in Angels, most agree that Angels are thought to have wings.

There have been many Angelic visitors throughout our evolution on this planet. Interestingly, the visitations that have been recorded in art and literature usually include the presence of wings and bright light.

What are wings? Why is there a consistent depiction throughout the ages of heavenly and sometimes not-so-heavenly human forms with wings? What is the concept of wings, and where did it come from?

True interdimensional travel does not require any conveyance, such as a "spaceship," as is so commonly accepted and highly dramatized on this planet. Shifting dimensions and traveling to other realms can be accomplished through a system of energy-portal openings. Each time there has been visual contact with those who have arrived here via a portal, the portal's light has reinforced the perception of "Angelic wings."

Many of us are still easily influenced by external stimuli and opinion. Commonly held belief systems are powerful. How often have you stopped doing something simply because the opinion of another dissuaded you? Perhaps you have tried a spiritual or mystical practice and did not initially feel or see anything. Did you then conclude that it is impossible? Perhaps you were confronting the power of your own subconscious belief systems. Perhaps you were being held in place, so to speak, by frozen imagination!

It is imagination that opens the doorways of perception. Your imagination is a great gift that can free you to manifest miracles in your life. Within the safety of your imagination you are able to transport yourself anywhere, and you have permission not to believe any of it!

We encourage you to allow yourself the complete and loving re-activation of your imagination. Imagine for a moment a long hallway of brilliant light. As you stare into this hallway, you see a Being emerge from the center of this light. Once this Being steps forward and is in full presence in front of you, the stream of light or the portal that is illuminating this Being from behind reveals a glowing and gentle presence. As the communication begins, the portal remains open, yet diminishes in size to hold the energy for the visitor while assisting the one who is witnessing to perceive more clearly.

The common artistic rendering of this portal translates as wings. Therefore, the acceptance of Angel wings appears to have evolved from a misinterpretation of the energy field, or portal, that was visible behind the visitor. This explains why there are also portrayals of dark visitors with wings.

The time is upon us to offer ourselves the gift of Angelic reconnection through a heightened vibrational state. The planet has undeniably increased its vibrational rate, and it is through this heightened vibration that we are able to bring forth the Galactic Yoga traditions. We are now at the time when anyone can ascend into the higher realms of consciousness with a bit of focus and dedication.

For centuries we have watched in awe as the mountain yogis came forth, offering miracles born of their methods of connection. In today's energy you can attain the Enlightened State of Being with a few months of dedicated focus, surrender, and trust.

At this time too, many false prophets will appear in mass numbers on the planet. As the heightened vibrational rate stirs longing for deeper connection, teachers and spokespersons can easily attract a following by capitalizing on the sincere longing of many. Are these spokespersons offering a true teaching? Or are they themselves deluded by the mysticism of a far-off land or mystery school? Do they engage your imagination? Are we not imagining a faraway land, with a mystical way of being?

Once again, imagination has served as a vehicle of opening. So in this time of false prophets and unlocked mysteries, how do you discern Truth? Only your heart, clear in the intent of Truth, can offer you this answer. Learning to listen and rely upon your heart is both a practice and a choice. You will not find your heart's truth in the opinions of others. You must discover for yourself the difference between the ego's desires and the true yearning for Union.

Many resist the heart, and resistance is a practice designed to continue the status quo. For example, the status quo accepts that Angels have wings. This is the interpretation of a human mind that was unable to clearly see beyond the immediate field of perception. Yet, we now know that these "wings" indeed are energy fields that offer transportation and protection. *Each of us has this ability and Divine Connection!*

Preoccupation with Angels is growing rapidly! Of course it is...because YOU are that!

WHAT IS AN ANGEL?

Ascended Non-matter Gloriously Expressing Light...and Love.

Your true Angelic connection has been dormant, and misinterpretations of what Angels are have led to the perpetuation of myths and stereotyping that supports only one way of being! Misinterpretation and myth result in many frightening experiences being played out in the cinema, and more are to come. Remember, in times of escalating energy, both the distortions and the Truth are stimulated.

The time of multidimensionality is now. As you allow yourself to accept that the world you have known has shifted, you will find your stability by remembering the truth of your Being. Let your Angelic truth step forward. With that single step, all becomes sane again.

When you are feeling chaotic, and when the messages of fear and destruction seem to be closing in on you, at that moment you are in the state of Angelic disconnect. This simply means that you have opened up a portal aligned with a chaotic Realm of existence. It does not mean that you are incapable of reopening your Angelic portal; rather, it is simply a reminder that you are well-practiced in aligning with the chaos!

This is the exact moment when you can stop, breathe, and activate your true Angelic presence. You can immediately shift the energy by *opening your wings* (see *Yogic practice on next page*). Remember to exercise your Angelic connection. The key is to interrupt the chaos by gifting yourself with reminders to shift your response. Perhaps now is a good time to put little sticky notes around your home that say *choose.*

When you are confronted with fear or stress, how do you respond? What is your automatic response now? There is always the moment of choice. How do you make it?

Enlightenment, or to be In-Light, is a state of being that exists with more tangible availability than ever before for those who choose to embrace it. Claim your truth as an Angelic Being of Love! Claim your power! There is no power that can stop the gift of Angelic presence when it has been activated to serve the expression of Light and Love. Empower your wings and fly again! You might just learn to delight in the gift of your imagination.

PRACTICE: FLAP AND CLAP

An Energy Expansion Exercise from the Galactic Yogic Teaching

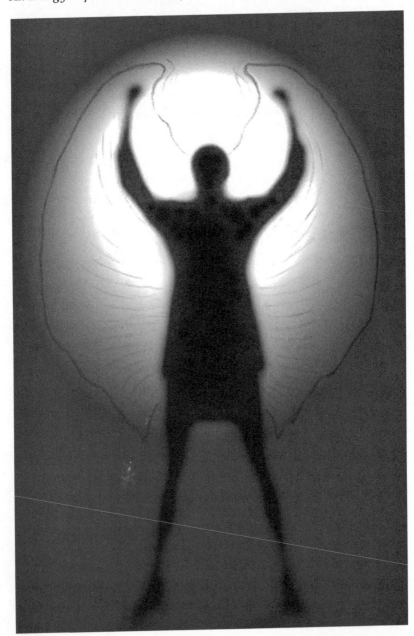

1. Stand as straight as possible with the feet slightly apart and with arms resting at your sides.
2. Close your eyes and take in a deep breath. Upon the exhale, open up a golden pyramid at the base of the spine and allow it to release infinity symbols up the spine.
3. Send the infinity symbols up into the center of the Lotus Chakra (approximately six inches above the head).
4. Keep breathing and visualize your wings behind you. Allow them to fully form. Focus upon the shape, color, and size.
5. Continue until the wings are well defined.
6. Open the eyes and relax the wrists by shaking them a few times.
7. Slowly begin to raise the arms with the wrists very relaxed. Bring the arms all the way up to the top of your wings, and allow the hands to initiate the downward motion once you have reached the top. *(See illustration, opposite page.)*
8. Repeat this at least three times.
9. When you are halfway down during the third repetition, bring the hands to the front of the heart center in prayer position. (Hands together, fingers pointed up.)
10. Take in a deep breath and upon the exhale, begin clapping.
11. Continue clapping, breathing, and yes, even smiling until you feel the energy completion.

It is optimal to repeat this process at least twice a day, and anytime you need to shift the energy you are experiencing. There is no limit to how many times a day you can repeat this process!

WHAT IS SOUL FOOD?

Just as you can't put jet fuel into a car, your body will not align with higher frequencies if you feed it with density realities. This includes the food you choose to ingest, the people you interact with, how you interact with your environment, literally everything!

Soul food offers a way of nourishing yourself that transcends the obligatory and guilt-ridden choices. Ask yourself the following question prior to any major decision that affects your soul destiny: Am I doing this because it serves my greater service, or am I doing it because I feel obligated?

Regardless of the answer to this question, you will be clear on your actions, and clarity is a primary building block of true soul nourishment. We are at the time when authenticity feeds the soul. Be honest with yourself.

Many wonder why we just can't transmute anything and everything we choose to release. Usually, it is because our body's environment has been bombarded with density to the point that we are numb. Whether we are truly transmuting, or simply wanting to believe we are, becomes an important discernment.

Soul Food relates to everything you set your eyes upon. Take a look around your home. If there is an object there that does not bring you Joy, it is time to give it away or at least box it up and store it for now. You can always revisit it later, if you need to. True harmony is nourishing. Be honest with yourself and your loved ones. Release within yourself the energy of doing something out of obligation and embrace joyful connections.

Nourishing your soul will always be conducive to maintaining a balanced existence. Your emotions will be in flow, your relationships will feel harmonious, and your Divine Connection will be beyond doubt. This is affirmation that your soul is aligned with your wonderful physical vessel, the body.

Soul food is also found through love. This love must begin with appreciation for the body. Whether your body is in the form of perfection as you see it or not, your love for this amazing home for the soul must be expressed. Practice unconditional love for your own body. The resulting nourishment will far exceed any other expression.

When the body knows that it is loved, an essential alignment with the soul has occurred. From this state of alignment, all that you wish to call forth does indeed manifest. Simply allow it to be so by being well fed!

Chapter Sixteen

2012: FOR OUR CHILDREN: THE DIVINE GALACTIC BLUEPRINT

> *What you call imagination is a doorway you*
> *have separated from by dismissing it as fantasy.*
> *Yet, your fantasies are simply the manifestation*
> *of energy seeking reunification through the filter*
> *of distortion. Free your imagination and the*
> *fantasy frees itself to appear in its wholeness.*
>
> ~ARCHANGEL ZADKIEL

How many times has the veil been lifted, and you considered it to be a dream? When you touch higher states of consciousness do you combine the Ascended Energy with density concepts in order to make them understandable to the human mind? Of course you do!

The Earth brain seeks to interpret which things fit where, using existing concepts as structure. Then, other people step in, who reword and reinterpret the intent, thus farther removing the listener from the pure stream of consciousness. It is OK to be wordless! Be the Truth, rather than the interpreter of Truth.

Why were we able to sustain and interact directly with otherworldly energies during the Atlantean period? How were we able to create DNA stranding that led to the creation of new life forms? What was the link that offered revelations about crystal energies and technologies that sustained life without taking from the planet on which we lived?

Many memories, and even more verifications, about our time in the first, or true, Atlantis have been gifted to us through the Archangelic Realm. Essentially, Atlantis was a bridge world. It existed in the fifth dimensional energy and we played with density. The very existence of Atlantis gave us the gift to keep traveling deeper into density.

When the Ascended Heart Chakra was revealed to us as the root center of a new chakra system, it became apparent that we were being prepared for something that was not currently on the planet. For thousands of years we had all been taught that the heart opening was the destination, the goal of spiritual practice. Suddenly, it was now the beginning, a doorway to something more.

This does not discount the teachings that have led us to the heart. They are necessary steps of preparation. All steps prior to the millennium were vital to open the doorway of energy that we are now embracing.

Yes! It can be difficult to wrap your mind around new revelations, and in an attempt to offer stability, it can easily discount them. However, when presented with the energetic evidence, coupled with the physical manifestations that are revealing themselves on our planet now, it becomes apparent that the *shift* is here.

At the cellular level, ALL beings on the planet are aware that a major shift is upon them. Preoccupation with ancient doomsday prophecies, Rapture agendas, even the New Golden Age of Peace and Harmony all have their origins in your DNA. Your cells know that you are here at the single most important time in our collective history, and your conscious mind wants details!

Archangel Zadkiel and the other messengers who have In-souled through Kira Raa all bring forth the same loving recognition. Too many details will displace your inner knowing and erode your self-trust. The Archangelic Realm truly realizes the Chinese proverb: *Give a man a fish and he'll eat for a day; teach a man to fish and he'll eat for a lifetime.*

ARCHANGEL ZADKIEL RESPONDS TO QUESTIONS

QUESTIONER: What are we preparing for? What is coming?

Whoa! Big question, is it not? [much laughter] We have offered you many insights on what is coming. The greatest gift we can give you is to know that what is coming for all six billion is the great gift of reunification. This is the time of your own evolution of density, of great reunification in a manner that has not been done before—and you are closely within this time. How each one of you experiences this is truly up to you. Each will be fulfilled in their own soul's recognition of this energy. Because of this, there are many energies that are available and present to you now.

How do you prepare? By recognizing the truth of your being and trusting your own heart. Each of you knows the truth of your heart; you know your answers. Trust them, trust yourself, trust your answers. If you cannot trust yourself, then love yourself for knowing this is where you begin. Remember not to judge yourself.

What is coming is still up to you. How you create it is in your own heart. Collectively, you will all have many similar experiences while you will also have many individual experiences. Dearest ones, so many come to us and say, "I want a date, a time, and place. I want it now, and unless you give this to me, I have nothing to listen to!"

*OK, this is fine. Those are the same ones who would have the date, the time, and the place, but then turn around and that would still not be good enough. It would still not open their hearts. **All the answers that we offer to you are to help you open up your own heart.***

We will share that you are now at a time of great, what many will call turmoil, and many will call Joy. It is simply where you choose to be. Many blessings.

QUESTIONER: You said that in the coming months there are going to be some changes happening. Natural disasters are already happening all over the world. Is there more concentration in one area or another, for instance the East Coast and the West Coast?

It is important to understand, dear one, that there will be many, many, many geographical changes. Pay attention to all that is happening. Follow the ley lines of the Earth. If you must look at what is happening, follow a ley line. See where it goes. Pay attention to the poles.

Pay attention to that which is happening. These answers you already know in your heart. The greatest thing for you to do is to pay attention. It is not easy, nor is it in our place, to give each one of you a specific day, time, or place. This is not of service. What is of service is for you to become aware. As you become aware and as you follow this preparatory time, what will happen is that you will be able to not only prepare yourselves through your own light of clarity, but all those around you will be prepared also. That is the great gift.

It is very simple to pluck days and times, but it does not serve the greater reunification of Light. With a day and time, your heart does not need to activate. All you need to do is dig your cave and get in it. We are not here to help you dig a cave. You must know that. We are here to help you open your heart and lift into the truth of your being; from there, your greater service is present. If you wish to dig a cave, there are many who will teach you.

*What we will teach you is how to **lift into your heart and above**, and truly be present for all without ever having to say a word. You make a difference just by being the truth of who you are. This is the honoring of light.*

*Make your choice. Make your decision and know where you want to be. Know and trust that you will be exactly where you need to be in any moment and time. Do not fear. Fear, dearest children, is what causes separation. **This time is not about fear—it is about Joy**. So take that one in.*

QUESTIONER: I understand in the reunification of all things that all beings received the gift of removal of karma. So what happens in the case of people doing bad things in the world? Do they have no karmic consequences for their actions?

This is a good question! Let us first of all share with you that there is not good or bad; there is only the judgment of what is good and bad. There is only that about which we are now on this planet saying, "Oh, I judge this to be spiritual," or "I judge this to be non-spiritual," or "I judge this to be good," or "I judge this to be bad." It is the same with the light and the dark.

All karma has been lifted. *What that means is that all souls are now free for reunification, but not all souls are choosing reunification in the same way.*

At the moment of reunification, every soul will be experiencing reunification based on completion of this experience in this realm of density and this time of expansion. So, not all souls will experience the same way, meaning some are now in light. Some are carrying light as Light-Bearers. Some are meant very much to hold torches on the path. There will be a time when so many will be on the path at once that they will be confused and have no idea where they are. This is why so many need to be Torchbearers. Those Torchbearers have already brought themselves forward.

All beings, without exception, are part of reunification. All souls as part of their completion in this time of reunification will go through a process which may, under the definition of the dogmatic understandings, look like they are still working out karma based on action.

So, where does all this bring us to? We have been asked by the Archangelic Realm not to offer interpretations of their messages. Rather, let each receive the message and bring it forth in their consciousness in the manner that best suits their own evolution. We have been offered a stairway home, an amazing energetic opening that is now available to all for the first time since the end-times of the first Atlantis.

THE DIVINE GALACTIC BLUEPRINT IS REVEALED

ARCHANGEL ZADKIEL: *The Divine Galactic Blueprint (The Ascended Chakra system) has been activated again. The last activation was at the culmination of your last experience in density, the end-time of Atlantis. It is important for you to recognize that the Divine Galactic Blueprint is back on the planet, and therefore you have the choice.*

You have the choice of saying, "I wish to participate in this energy. I wish to be part of the lifting, and I will indeed touch the door of consciousness and bring to light the greatest manifestation that I can." Or you can say, "Not for me!" Either way, this is good, because you have made a choice.

Making your choice is the most important gift you can give the world.

When we say the world, we do not mean just the planet here. We say world, and you all think Earth. No. The world is much larger than that which has a little bit of land and ocean, and on which you currently live. It is much larger. Soon, all the worlds will fold in upon one another, and the intermingling and truth of the strands of time will be released, opened, celebrated, and integrated. Oh yes, that was a mouthful. There is much there to understand!

The Divine Galactic Blueprint has been opened as the energy on the planet is ready for greater alignments now. You are in the energy of being a conscious co-creator. You are at the time of culminating conscious co-creation, or conscious chaos, whichever you choose to experience.

The questions arising now that your consciousness is coming into fullness are: How do you move forward? What do you want to do with this Energy Upliftment?

It is important for you to remember that what you do with the energy brings you to a higher level. We use the word "higher" only to offer you a frame of reference. It will bring you to a higher level of conscious connection, conscious understanding, conscious being, conscious knowing and expressing. How you express through the Divine Galactic Blueprint is offered in the following steps.

The Divine Galactic Blueprint is an extension of the traditional chakra system that was explored earlier in this book. It opens portals of connectivity and beingness that are well beyond the understandings of the third dimension. If you find yourself seeking greater understanding of this

Ascended Chakra system, there are many Archangelic teachings about the Divine Galactic Blueprint found at www.SelfAscension.com.

EXPRESSING THE DIVINE GALACTIC BLUEPRINT

There is a way of living, the Enochian way. There are Twelve Torches that lead to the steps of the Ascension Portals which are available on this planet. It is all available now. It is simply a question of understanding and reintegrating the energies to do this. There are those of you who wish to lift.

Often we hear, "I want to leave with my body;" "I don't want to leave with my body." "How do I leave?" "How does it happen?"

My goodness! Hang out and have some fun right now! You'll be leaving soon enough! Yes! You will experience it in the manner in which your consciousness has stepped into that experience. Some of you may very well feel as if you are, indeed, stepping into another realm with your body. Others will feel very comfortable saying, "Why am I bringing this body along?"

It is OK! It does not have a definite response. So many wish to tell you, "You can only go this way. You can only ascend this way." No!

You have already Ascended! Take that in.

If you had not already Ascended, you would not be prepared to do what you are getting ready to do as a collective humanity now.

Only in the realm of the first, second, and third densified chakras do you believe that you have not already Ascended. As you move into the Divine Galactic Blueprint, you allow yourself to fully integrate upward. Stop sending cords into the planet!

When they tell you to ground your energy, immediately go into the heart chakra, which is the root of the Ascended State, and ground there! It will lift you up! It will bring you into the energetic alignment principle of Divine lifting.

The energy of the Truth can only be present when you ground your energy in the heart of the Ascended State.

You say, "Maybe, maybe not!" What is important for you to understand is that as we move into this chakra, as we move into Divine Seeing, as we move into the recognition of Oneness and Truth, this opens up! This is the lunar module of the expanded crown, which is the next chakra within the Divine Galactic Blueprint.

THE EXPLODED CROWN CHAKRA

Within the traditional system, the crown chakra is at the top of the head. In the Ascended State of the Divine Galactic Blueprint, your crown chakra is actually three points of energy.

The top point is approximately six inches above your head, and then there is one to the right, and one to the left. Together they form the base of a pyramid of energetic light that includes your third eye, and these three points. These are the four points of the base. Let us review the entire system so far, before we go forward.

(We have inserted a diagram below to help with visual understanding. The Bottom Point is the third eye, and the surrounding three points are the "exploded crown.")

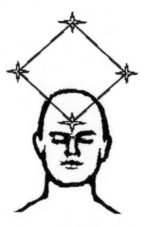

The root of this system is your heart chakra, which is two Divine intersecting spirals of emerald green and gold. Move to the truth chakra (former throat chakra), which is an aquamarine. It is the beautiful emerald green that comes up and meets with that which was formerly blue, and turns into aquamarine, thereby offering great Truth and connectivity.

Next you have the third eye, which is an opalescent pearl of two Divine intersecting infinity swirls. From here, go six inches above the head to discover the top point of the new crown, which also has a point to the right and a point to the left. It's like a helmet.

Understand that this helmet brings you into great lifting energy. It brings the opportunity for Divine Connection. You cannot expand, or we prefer to use the word explode, your current crown chakra unless you have truly released, cleared, gotten rid of, and said, "OK, enough already!" to the first three traditional lower chakras.

It is very important that you no longer have all that activity going on in those first three chakras. It is important. So many say, "Oh, I am above this teaching! I am that teaching! I cannot do this! I cannot do that! I already know this; I already know that!" Good! Very good! Then live in your heart and move up. When you need to declare that you have an understanding of something, when the ego comes back in and says, "Oh, don't do this!" or "You must do that!" it is a wondrous time to reflect and observe, "Which chakra am I in now?"

Dearest ones, recognize more than ever that the lower three chakras are there. They want to keep you on the planet. They say, "Please send cords to Mother Earth. Please keep me here; I don't want to go." This is especially apparent when the heart embraces intersecting Divine spirals of infinite energy. It is important for you to recognize that this is how you will lift. You must see the entire Divine Galactic Blueprint to understand the recognition of the energy that has come in.

THE ENTRANCE OF THE FIFTH, SEVENTH, AND NINTH DIMENSIONS

Look at your Earth now, and visualize a second Earth. Simply edit, copy, paste, and make another one right next to it. Good! Now what happens? It's a little off-center from the first one, not quite on. It may look the same, but they are not quite together.

It is important for you to understand that the fifth, seventh, and ninth dimensions are clamoring to come back into Oneness with you now.

There are many of you who will not go to the fifth dimension.

You will go to other dimensions.

You are not limited by that which the mind of the brain of the human vessel wishes to create! So, moving the Earth into the fifth dimension **has to** happen.

It cannot not happen. You cannot **not** shift. **How** you shift—that is your decision. That is your opportunity. This is why you need a helmet, because some of you will go crashing into it for sure. Some of you will be bearers of light that will hold open the portal for others to understand and move forward. All seven Ascension Portals on the planet are activated; it is the time of the **full** activation!

It is important for you to understand that as each of these seven portals are increasingly activated, which activate seven more, which are activated by seven more, each of you will be drawn to align with the portal that resonates with your energy.

Many of you will move your homes, and many of you have just moved. Many of you are thinking, "Oh, not again. I thought I was set!" You **are** "set." The Divine Galactic Blueprint has come in to offer you the opportunity to reconnect with the truth that you are.

A portal of light has come in around you and said, "Lift, go up, do!" As you embrace your expanded crown, as you move into the true vision of the opalescent pearl, as you understand that you can indeed walk into the portal, you find that it is more and more complicated to stay anchored in density.

Know this. Some of you may say, "Why am I bumping into things all the time?" Well, you are just not here that often! OK. No big deal. Some of you may say, "I miss every appointment there is." Good, you're on Angel Time. It is important to recognize that, more and more, you will be releasing many of the density traps. They will become apparent, much more apparent, especially as you practice going into the expanded crown energies. Go into your helmet.

Take a moment now and reflect upon the Ascension Acceleration Energy Experiences that were discussed in Chapter 10. Most likely, as you first encountered them, you found that you were having many if not all of these experiences in response to the times at hand. They may have immediately brought to mind a friend or relative who is experiencing some or all of the AAEEs. The plain truth is that MANY people have been experiencing these energies, and MOST do not know what they are or how to respond to them.

The crown energy is expanding, and is most commonly felt as head pressures, hearing high-pitched tones in the ears, and vision changes. How you choose to respond to these experiences is a personal and important decision. Allow yourself to float with these experiences the next time they surface. Perhaps try something as simple as asking your body to speak to you during that moment of connection, and then TRUST YOURSELF and the answers you receive.

RESPONSE TO THE SHIFTING ENERGIES

As you connect with the energy of the "expanded crown," you will become more aware of vibrational sound shifts. These sound shifts are happening within you and in the outer world. In fact, our Earth is also experiencing these shifts in the form of earthquakes. There will be more sonic information and bombardment to the planet. So you must pay attention.

Know that the energy of the Divine Galactic Blueprint expands, stabilizes, and comes back in! It is important for you to recognize that it is not a stagnant energy. As you resolve the issues of the lower three chakras, then the energy that begins in your heart goes up—it lifts. It then offers a base point for this expanded crown, where the energy goes in many directions. Here is where you touch galactic knowingness! This is where interdimensional knowing comes into consciousness. To realign with infinite expansion, you must resolve, release, and declare, "I've done it, had it, been there," concerning attachment to the first three chakras!

It is important for you to resolve your attachment in these chakras. Otherwise, you will remain in the playground of power struggles.

RECONNECTING WITH
YOUR DIVINE GALACTIC BLUEPRINT

ARCHANGEL ZADKIEL: *At the end-times of Atlantis, many of you were fully activated in your Divine Galactic Blueprint and it gave you great energy. What you perceive in this time now to be unusual information, advanced scientific, technological, or DNA revelations, was the complete embracing of the Divine Galactic Blueprint, which is here for you now.*

*You have entered into the integration now as conscious co-creators. **Joyous** lifting, **joyous** reintegration, recognition of great truth, and the beginning of knowing how to do it again, is upon you in this moment. This time, you are awake with responsible co-creative energy, for this was your agreement when Atlantis ended! You made an agreement to be here, now. You declared that you would be present, remember, and embrace the true alignment of the Divine Galactic Blueprint. You committed to the prevention of its misuse, and annihilation.*

Congratulate yourself! You are Here, and you are Remembering.

Many of you in the time of Atlantis took responsibility energy and converted it to me energy. How do we accelerate one piece? There were indeed vessels that had different forms of energy in them. There was indeed a distinction between who should and who shouldn't embrace galactic understanding.

This does not exist here now. All six billion of you are able to connect, for all six billion are connected. All six billion will receive the same energies. The question is, how do you move forward with them? Know this, and pay attention!

Many say, "Oh, my goodness! I have so many good options, and all these options feel good! How do I choose?"

First, go into the root, which is the heart chakra, and simply allow yourself to call in a Divine Ray of Connectivity. We call this the heart highway. When your heart highway opens and the Divine Ray of Connectivity comes in, in that moment, the only option will be before you.

When you have more than one option before you, you must know that your first three chakras are still factoring in, because indeed, dearest children, your purest truth is always abundantly clear, and all other things fall away.

When you feel ready, claim the opening of the expanded crown; then you will Divinely see, and you will know.

*Trust, dearest children! You already trust or you would not be here. The level of your trust is another question! The more you **trust**, the more you love. Remember, in the Realm of the Archangelic, **trust and love are the same thing; there is no difference.***

There is only one thing that destroys love, dearest ones, and it is lack of trust. Remember that you must trust yourself! As you love yourself and trust yourself, everything becomes abundantly clear, and you understand the Divine Unfoldment.

Doubt, dearest children, is the only other thing that can take you away from the truth of consciousness. How many of you have ever known, without a doubt, something about yourself that made you feel inspired, connected, in your power? Then someone whispers something to you and you reconsider your knowing. "Oh, my goodness! Who am I to claim this about me?" The doubt took it away!

Doubt is the only thing that can take away your power. It is the only thing. You are in the energy of the Divine Galactic Blueprint! The Elohimian lifestyle, the Enochian[63] way, the Twelve Torches to the steps of Ascension are here! They are being revealed to you now! Dearest children, the only thing that can stop you from walking them is doubt. Trust yourself. Know your heart.

A PRACTICE

To activate your Divine Galactic Blueprint, we recommend that you practice thirty days of releasing. Go into the Ascended Heart and ask to release whatever is clinging in the first three chakras. Simply breathe deeply and command that these attachments be released. Pay attention to what you experience.

This is very important for you, so pay attention. Much will show up. Your attachments are here in density, so they will appear. It is also important to release "judgment." When the Archangels talk about trust, when they talk about doubt, and living in the stream of the pillars of light, some say, "Hmmmm..." This is a judgment, a touch of skepticism, is it not? How do your automatic judgments limit you?

ARCHANGEL URIEL[64]: *Remember, there is no old way and there are no new ways; there are no old energies and there are no new energies. There is only energy! You create separation with words, dearest children. You set yourselves apart from others. How can you truly be of service to the world if you set yourself apart from others by feeling you are among the elite in your beliefs? It then separates you from those whom you believe you are superior to.*

Dearest children, the opportunity to step fully into your Divine Galactic alignment is now. Pay attention to your rest. Some of you may have very interrupted sleep patterns, especially during the thirty days of release. Know these interruptions are because of the openings that are occurring on a galactic level. You are aligned with these energies; you are an indispensable part of it all!

Know how loved you are. The time you have waited for is here. Have fun! Activate! As you consciously activate your Divine Galactic Blueprint, you hold energy for thousands more.

Each one of you activating just to this level offsets 100,000 others. One hundred thousand, on this planet! If you ever doubt how important you are, just remember that.

When you make this choice in consciousness, you lift 100,000 with you. Help others make this choice, and if they say "no," accept their path as perfect for them. There is no loss, for they are integrated into your hundred thousand.

We love you dearly and honor your journey as the Travelers.

FOR OUR CHILDREN: YOUR CHOICES MATTER AND YOU DO MAKE THE DIFFERENCE!

It is important to understand that all things are held in an energetic balance. As the polarity increases on Earth, what seems to be a tension here is in fact a new form of balance when viewed from afar. The tension within the earthly realm offers energy to its inhabitants. It is also important to understand that a person holding a frequency of unconditional love balances or offsets the energetic pull of 100,000 holding the energy of fear. Thus, 60,000 people holding the energy of unconditional love balance the energetic impact of 6 billion caught in the illusion of fear. This is yet another reason to never doubt the power of your heart!

When the Divine Galactic Blueprint first came in, we did not initially realize the depth of the teaching it offered. The information above is very powerful and far deeper than one might realize on the first read-through. Yet there is much more to be revealed. The Divine Galactic Blueprint offers an entire cosmology, the opportunity to access many dimensions. There is much more teaching available on this that is beyond the scope of this book. The information shared in this chapter is powerful, for not only are clues offered with respect to the energetic pathway back to Source, but also for how to live in the world! This information is of great importance for the souls known as the Travelers, for the Divine

Galactic Blueprint opens a roadmap for the journey home. However, as Archangel Zadkiel points out, the Divine Galactic Blueprint cannot be activated if one is preoccupied with the density chakras of safety, sex, and power.

In future books we will be sharing more on how to use the energy of the Divine Galactic Blueprint to access other dimensions. For now, it is mainly important to assimilate the basic understanding that the Heart is the foundation of the Ascended State, and then resolve the density dramas of the lower three chakras. To avail oneself of the Self-Ascension opportunity culminating in 2012, one must release Density Consciousness and grow into Ascension Awareness while having already navigated through Spiritual Activism. From this stratum of consciousness, the teachings gain new relevance and are understood with an awareness that is simply not present inside of either Density Consciousness or Spiritual Activism. The path grows richer with your commitment and trust.

Every action you take in this moment, now, is also impacting our children. Recently we received an e-mail from a high school guidance counselor in California, asking if we could please come and reassure the students they would not all be dead in a few years. The impact of the media, prophetic interpretations, and gossip, along with Hollywood sensationalism, are disturbing to our children. These outer-world energies are compounded by your own fears. If you are in anxiety, the children will be impacted. Are they not looking to you for guidance and positive action?

Children are sensitive to the energy of their surroundings. If there is free-floating anxiety in the environment, they will be affected. Talk with your children. Help them to understand that the world is releasing old energies and that there is nothing to fear. Most importantly, release fear from your own life! Do the spiritual practices that restore balance and peace to you.

If you were uncomfortable with the recognition that the karmic imperative has been released, perhaps it was because it stirred within you the need to release attachment and apathy. It is the collective apathy of Density Consciousness, in conjunction with attachments, that feeds the fear that is stimulating nightmares, poor school performance, and emotional instability in our schoolchildren. We have empowered one number, 2012, with unnecessary anxiety.

It is time for each of us to get clear. Are you at peace with your choices? Let your consciousness awaken to the greater truth of your existence, and walk through the Pyramid of Authenticity with integrity as your lodestar. From there, the Divine Galactic Blueprint opens and fear dissipates. Is it to be our legacy that our children were afraid to live because of a looming doomsday prophecy? Or perhaps our legacy is that we decided to choose to be at peace with our own hearts and claim our empowerment by saying yes to ourselves.

There is only the Now,
and the soon-to-be Now.

~ARCHANGEL ZADKIEL

Chapter Seventeen

WALKING ON WATER
WHILE THE EARTH SHAKES

> The cycles of Matter will be succeeded by
> Cycles of Spirituality and a fully developed
> mind... the majority of the future mankind
> will be composed of glorious Adepts.
>
> ~HELENA BLAVATSKY[65]

This journey began in Chapter One with a simple question:
Are you ready to fully awaken from the dream?

You are eternally shifting, moving, and creating anew: over and over and over again.

What if it just keeps repeating, the whole cycle, until you get it? What if we have already done this? Archangel Zadkiel has consistently provided the message that everything we are experiencing now has been done by us before, including the process of awakening. We return to our Ascended Consciousness to assist ourselves, and others, in offering service to as many as possible.

Are you willing to listen? Are you ready to discern your inner truth and make a conscious decision?

Gifting yourself with the many practices that have been offered, combined with simple acceptance of your beingness without judgment, will offer your brain great clarity, your heart the capacity to discern the Truth, and your soul the answers you seek. Let us gently remind you once again that cultivating a conscious connection with your heart's wisdom offers value to everyone, regardless of their beliefs or level of consciousness.

Make your own decisions about the meaning of the information you have read here. Let this book help you ground more fully in your own heart by showing you what you will trust and what you will not. We celebrate your ability to know what is right for you at this time.

Is this the great split?

Does 2012 start it all over again?

Or, does 2012 offer an Ascension opportunity to those who are ready, and leave the rest to cycle farther into density expansion? There is no guidebook for this time. There are clues left behind by Mayan visionaries, Hopi Elders, and interpretations of the Bible's Book of Revelation. These works offer some perspectives and perhaps even some reassurance if we can correlate them with our own intuitive understandings.

The Divine expresses itself in many ways, and in all ways remembers all expressions, all that is. As an expression of God, you have these characteristics of understanding and components of the whole. You have traveled far from Source, and as you return to that birthplace you awaken to yourself, to your Divine inheritance. Thus your heart will help you filter out density perspectives from Truth.

The ego challenges re-union with a false sense of individuation. The ego loves drama and self-aggrandizement; thus it will be attracted to false memory. The ego loves experts and also judges them harshly. We are collectively reunifying, blending, and reclaiming memory. It is important to become a conscious co-creator, **to re-member with consciousness.**

You don't need a guidebook that offers you a new biology of spirit or a roadmap to follow. All you need is the recognition that you have done this all before (*the definition of Self-Ascension*), and trust in your Ascended Heart. Stay connected to your inner guidance and practice keeping your eyes on the Divine at all times. With this focus and surrender you can dissolve the hypnotic grip of Density Consciousness and claim your empowered mastery.

Unlike in prior centuries, the vibrational level of the planet is now supporting the uplifting of consciousness and reunification in a way that has never existed or been available before. Self-realization or enlightenment (*to be In-Light*) is available to all right now. People worldwide are awakening to their spiritual authenticity.

The Divine has opened the portals, forgiven our debts, and invited us home. This is the time of Grace, when all you need to do is say a resounding YES. There are no required credentials, no penance to be paid, no suffering required—you have done that all before as well. This is why Archangel Zadkiel reminds us often to simply say YES and to dance in circles of Joy! The energy of YES opens, affirms, and makes us available to the gift of the Ascending Energies.

PRACTICE RECAP: TRUSTING THE FIRST YES

The power of learning to hear and trust the answers from your heart is a primary one. Here are some steps to assist you in enhancing this practice:

Always begin with simple questions, and you may wish to have fun by creating affirmative statements with known answers, such as, I am a woman, or I am a man, etc. The value of these types of declarations is to uncover any hidden energies that may wish to create false answers within.

If you are accustomed to using a pendulum or other dowsing device, put it down while you do this practice. Your ability to call forth clear responses will only enhance any dowsing skills when you use them again.

Clearly, this is training, so be patient. You may wish to create an atmosphere that supports your quietude—perhaps lighting a candle, creating a quiet space, providing the body physical comfort, etc.

Writing down your questions and declarations ahead of time also assists the mind to focus on responses only, rather than the creation of the questions.

Ready?

1. Take in a deep cleansing breath and exhale with noise. Repeat as many times as needed to feel completely open.
2. Read your first declaration as a means to open the stream of consciousness.
3. Be completely present with your knowing, or inner voice.
4. You have already received the first answer. Did you hear it? Did you feel it?
5. If yes, breathe again, and continue.
6. If no, ask again, and be alert.
7. Regardless of whether you heard the answer or not, take a moment to observe your reaction to the answer. The answer received in clarity may not be the one the brain desires, so it becomes simple to tune it out.
8. Practice often, for trusting the "yes" from our hearts means we are simultaneously releasing years of distractions.

The completion energy will lift you as you say YES! to it. Enlighten-ment can be a step-by-step process, a Quantum Leap, or both. Accept that you have completed the preparatory steps. You are at the time, as all are, in which the opportunity for a Quantum Leap is upon you. Will you allow yourself new understandings? Will you accept a new way of being?

With 2012 rapidly approaching, when the opportunity to take the Quantum Leap appears, will you be able to recognize it? Have you resolved your attachments enough to lift off the game board?

As ARCHANGEL ZADKIEL HAS STATED SO CLEARLY: *The secret is not so much in the knowing as it is in the Being.*

When one is being, then one understands. If one is allowing, if one is in surrender, then one can be. When one has the secret, it means that they are still withholding from themselves, from others, from the world. There is no basis for this withholding unless one desires power or control. The Elohim does not desire power or control; this is why there can be no secret. The only gift that the Elohim offers is the expanding Love of Light. That is the big secret!

That is the great secret. Unlock the floodgate to the heart, and allow the torrent of unconditional love for the Self to come in. Forgive, and re-emerge as the soul-based, heart-centered, Self-Ascended Energy, ready to be of service to all.

Be in the continuous flow of the God of Love.

EMBRACE THE NOW

Linear time results when you separate yourself from Unity. It is as if you are standing outside the circle of unity. As you separate, the edges of the circle seem to fall away, leaving you with a sense of past, present, and future.

We are folding time. You cannot witness the fullness of Truth unless you stand inside the timeless portal, where all is known now. Everything outside the portal is linear, where the wholeness of the Truth is just a concept and not an experience. Simply moving around the portal (circle) recreates linear structures and thinking; therefore, you must go within to perceive the wholeness.

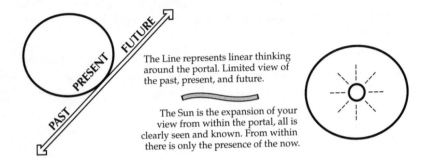

The Line represents linear thinking around the portal. Limited view of the past, present, and future.

The Sun is the expansion of your view from within the portal, all is clearly seen and known. From within there is only the presence of the now.

PORTAL THINKING

As you navigate the portal circles in the diagram, if you take the line of linear thinking and simply bring the two ends together, they become wholeness. From wherever you are, you can be in the center. It is your time to stand in the center and fully embrace your Star Consciousness. From this center, *from your centered-ness*, all is visible. There is no time; there is simply the Ecstatic Being of the endless now.

Your mind is your servant, not your master. It is time to restore your mastership with loving recognition of the many gifts your mind has offered to you. It is time to stand in the center by making your choice to be there.

ASCENSION FREQUENCIES

Times have certainly changed. It is indeed the time of transfiguration and transformation. We have entered the gap between two worlds. From 2001 to 2012 is a period of rapid escalation and reorganization of energy. Your vibrational rate is increasing, as is the rate of everyone on the Earth.

This heightened energy is evidenced through the increased polarity on the Earth. Old social structures are collapsing from within and failing to perform, political structures no longer meet the needs of the whole, and health issues increase as our bodies are not given the support they need to assimilate the new frequencies. People are medicating more because conventional science cannot offer an empirical explanation for their symptoms. That is, you cannot diagnose Ascension! There are no clinical protocols to use to help isolate the symptomology and energy frequencies! *(Revisit the AAEE list on page 125.)*

Self-Ascension is an exercise in trust. Trust will walk you through the process, and there is no other way to expand into the love that you are. You cannot think your way through a vibrational shift. Thought can help you understand the process as you walk to the doorway. However, Trust is the energy that lifts you beyond the limitations of the known and into the limitless expansiveness of true Being.

CLAIM YOUR MASTERY

Yes, you do have a choice! Many choices must be made along the path. Life on Earth gives you countless opportunities to stray from your essence, and each time you stray you must choose again. Mastery involves noticing when you are distracted, being grateful for that realization, dissolving any judgments that flared up, and then recommitting to your surrender to Spirit. Surrender is the active form of trust.

If you choose to live a conscious life, know that it is a full-time commitment. This is more than a weekly meeting kind of commitment. It is daily surrender, an hourly choice and moment-by-moment recognition. It will get easier as you allow it to be.

Many are in the habit of the habit of the pain of the pain. This is the result of having swallowed an unhealthy dose of Density Consciousness. It's not just that you live in a world of mass illusion and fear; it's that as you awaken, you judge yourselves harshly for being addicted to the density illusion, thus creating more separation and pain. *(See event-response loop, page 84.)*

How often have you felt that you were missing something? How often have you felt that you had done something wrong, that you needed help or forgiveness? How often have you felt inadequate in some way? How often have you felt confused, depressed, tired, or lonely?

All of these experiences result from being in the habit of the pain. All of these experiences are habits that are deepened by judging ourselves and others. As you release yourself from the habits, your energy field expands and you'll attract more loving experiences to you.

As the energy escalation leading to 2012 heightens polarity, Density Consciousness will invite greater disconnection and pain. Remind yourself that this is just a habit seeking to consume your attention. If you are in the habit of recognizing your identity in your ego instead of in your soul, then you are also in the habit of depending upon outside authorities or influences. Yet, if you yearn for Union you are being pulled in two directions, an uncomfortable situation indeed.

Make your choice in either direction, and your commitment will resolve the pain. It does not matter which choice you make as long as you truly align with it. All choices offer resolution.

Each year between now and 2012 will support your unfolding mastery. You can use the increasing energy to become polarized and deeply entrenched in a point of view, or you can use the energy to Ascend, to be in the world but not of the world. Either decision is acceptable. Know, though, that this is not a decision that can be put off for long; indecision is the energy of density. If you fail to make your commitment to practice mastery daily, then by default you will be drawn into Density Consciousness, and a decision has, in fact, been made.

IT DOESN'T MATTER WHAT YOU THINK OR SAY

Your thoughts and your words are meaningless. They will not lift you into your Ascended Heart and above. Thoughts and words are playthings. Your intentions, your love emanation, and your actions are how you will be known.

We are all immersed in a sea of Density Consciousness. It is your light that lifts you. When the fifth-dimensional world peels away from the third-dimensional Earth, there will be many who align with the third dimension whom you might have thought would have ascended.

In fact, their energetic alignment was with the 3-D world, regardless of their words. It is possible that those who stayed in the third-dimensional expression were victims of their own form of self-deception. Self-deception is a pitfall that can seduce any of us; it is the ego painting a spiritual picture that distracts us from our true soul alignment. Or, it is possible that those who chose the third-dimensional alignment did so out of a desire to be of Boddisattvic service to those souls who were unaware of the choice. We cannot judge. Indeed, the remaining third-dimensional experience will have many Torchbearers to assist others with their subsequent awakening, and many will continue to Self-Ascend from the Earth in the years from 2012-2024.

The path of enlightenment is the path on which one surrenders the dominance of the ego. Enlightened Beings have not eliminated their egos; their egos are simply at rest. As long as you have a body you will have an ego. Therefore, making peace with your ego is prerequisite to being able to make soul-based decisions.

ARE YOU THE PILLAR OR A TORCH?

Question: You have talked about being a Pillar of Light and at other times you have stated that many are called to be Torchbearers. What is the difference between a Torchbearer and a Pillar of Light? How do you know which one you are?

ARCHANGEL ZADKIEL: *It is important to remember, dearest ones, that there are many, many pathways of light and many expressions of light. We are at the time when all pathways are being fulfilled. This is why your manifestation abilities have become so large and are so quickly fulfilled. Pay attention to what you are focusing upon because everything is expanding.*

Some are saying, "Oh, is that why everything is getting so big?" Yes, you are able to manifest very quickly, instantaneously, so you must pay attention to where your focus is.

Dearest ones, as a Torchbearer you walk with all. A Torchbearer carries the torch and walks among. A pillar is an anchor of light that keeps the path illuminated. There is a great distinction between the two. Both offer equilateral service; both offer a way out of darkness.

There are many who ask about relatives or friends whom they feel are in pain with density, and want to know how to help them. Hold the torch for them. There are times when you may be both the torch and the pillar. You may be a pillar in this moment, and very shortly thereafter you may become a walking pillar, which is a torch.

It is not that you are one or the other. You simply have the opportunity to decide. When is it best to be a Pillar emanating light so that one can see the path, and when is it best to be the Torchbearer who is walking with and helping others to keep going?

Dearest children, how do you know? Go into your heart. Ask yourself, "Where am I of greatest service in the expression of my light? Where can I manifest?" Look at your own manifestation. Look around you, look where you live, look at your associations, look at your daily life. If you are not happy, then you have not surrendered it all to God and you are truly not observing.

Make your choice. Where do you choose to align your energies? Where do you want to be? Living in the fifth dimension or the third? It is that simple. Be the Torchbearer, be the Pillar, or be both. Know the difference, recognize the discernment, and walk forward. You are at a time when you are able to cultivate greater miracles than have ever happened before. Why is it that miracles have become so common that they are not enough? They happen all the time, and yet many yawn and say give me more.

Dearest children, you are a miracle; your presence is a great miracle. Are you a Torchbearer or are you a Pillar? You are All… how do you choose to express?

Without a Torchbearer nearby, many will easily be seduced by the illusion. Simply being in the truth of your own soul's expression sends a light that benefits all. Know the true power of your Ascended Heart.

YOU ARE THE GURU

We all need teachers from time to time, and we serve the greater good by teaching others from time to time. The key to effective teaching is not to open your mouth unless asked a question! This distinguishes an act of service from gossip and one-upmanship. Unsolicited commentary is usually just ego banter. If a person asks for help in reaching clarity or discerning guidance, then an opportunity to serve another has arisen.

A good therapist or teacher will help you trust yourself and find your inner compass. The pitfall is that some teachers and therapists are aligned with belief systems that are birthed from Density Consciousness. Thus, while they offer emotional support, they also offer another refinement of the density limitation.

This can be helpful as we learn to cope better with conventional living. It is also helpful to create a sense of competence in addressing life's challenges, and that is as far as it goes. When you decide it is time to set aside ego evolution in favor of Ascension Consciousness, your priorities will shift, as will your teachers. So get clear on what your choice is. Is it conventional empowerment, or is it spiritual in-lightenment that you want?

You have almost finished reading this book. Thus, you are seeking a level of experience that is beyond emotional quietude. You are seeking true Union, true Peace. When we seek to rise from the stream of Density Consciousness, we do need a Torchbearer to show the way. It is as if your being has been swept downstream in a river. Someone needs to be on shore to extend their hand and help lift you out. Their light helps you find your own light. It is the reason we are all here: To provide All with the opportunity to reunify with their own light by simply being present with ours. Ask for guidance, listen, and you will be led.

It is up to you to find the doorway to inner communion. It is up to you to listen to that communion. It is up to you to take action based upon that listening. These three steps—find, listen, and act—are yours alone.

Once you find your path, commit to it. With your inner communication channel open, you'll know the difference between the light and shades of density. You'll know, because you are the Guru! And, as you catch yourself knowing and being this truth, let a smile appear. This is the Bliss of Conscious Beingness.

TIME OF CULMINATION

The year 2012 represents a date on the calendar. It is an estimated "boiling point" in mass consciousness. It is not so much a cosmic deadline as it is the arrival of a critical mass in consciousness. The image of raising the temperature in a pot of water is quite appropriate.

When does water actually boil? As the heat increases in a pot of water, little bubbles begin to form and rise to the surface. As the temperature continues to increase, more and more little bubbles rise. At some point these bubbles combine into a large mass rising, a rolling boil. Those who have lifted from the water have undergone a phase shift—they have become steam. The water is still present in the vapor—it is just a lot less dense.

The temperature of consciousness, so to speak, has been rising for some years. Since the release of karma, the heat has steadily increased. Little bubbles are starting to rise, and those bubbles represent the people who choose to activate their full awakening now. We anticipate that in the coming three years, more and more people will lift off the game board of Earth school and anchor in the fifth-dimensional energies.

Those who have found their way to other dimensions will illuminate the path for many. In fact, we believe that by the year 2012 more people will have realized Enlightenment than ever before in the history of the planet. Thousands of people holding Ascension Consciousness at that time will offer an energetic balance to those who are holding on to polarized positions. This provides a balancing energy for all to have their culminating experience.

Remember, it is the various levels of consciousness that stimulate discernment about your own choices. While you are in a body on the Earth, you often need a mirror in order to call forth your awareness. It is the wide contrast in ways of being that helps us to understand our own choices. Be grateful for them all. The teacher needs the student just as much as the student needs the teacher. We are interdependent.

We are traveling on this journey together. During the coming years, more and more people will affiliate with their soul groups. More and more people will find themselves drawn to associations based upon soul energy. The universe is "raising the temperature," and we are reorganizing ourselves, preparing for the phase shift.

We are in a time of culmination, and as the karmic imperative has been lifted, a time of powerful co-creation is upon us. This Divine challenge and privilege offers you an opportunity to expand beyond all perceived limitations and experience the Joy of Ascension Consciousness.

ENTERING THE FIFTH DIMENSION NOW

The fifth dimension is a state of resonance that can coexist with the world of the third dimension. You will recognize it through a felt sense. Fifth-dimensional energies are indeed of a higher frequency and are within reach of everyone here.

Moving from density and anchoring in fifth-dimensional energy takes discipline and focus. The sea of third-dimensional consciousness washes over us at every opportunity. To anchor in the fifth dimension means that you have anchored your energy into your Ascended Heart Chakra and have connected your heart with your expanded crown chakra of the Divine Galactic Blueprint. This experience anchors with Ascension Awareness.

Holding your energy in your heart and expanded crown chakra will result in your taking an observer point of view more often. Instead of being a reactive, unconscious participant in an unfolding drama, you will be watching the unfolding interactions with less concern and immersion. You'll have a different sense or feeling. This a solid sign that you are in fact in a different place.

As you further release judgment, you offer acceptance and freedom to all, without any limits, It is from this place that you can be at peace with the interpersonal squabbling, global wars, and dramas of those who are acting out in front of you. Even those family members who try their best to guilt-trip you into density-based interactions cannot disturb your peace. With one breath they will accuse you of being too detached or apathetic about important issues, and in the next breath they will admire your clarity and seek your counsel! You are then "in the world and not of the world."

Once you begin living in the higher chakras of your Divine Galactic Blueprint, the habitual lens of perception can still operate. You may initially see the same outer world. You will notice some new inner sensations and yet the outer world will look familiar. This is partially due to your habitual lens of perception and partially due to the fact that the third dimension is overlaid with the fifth dimension. It is a superimposed picture. Which part are you looking at?

What you attend to determines what you miss! Start to notice your feelings more. Not your emotions—*your felt sense of things*. As you cultivate this felt sense of things, you'll begin to notice that the backdrop of your experience shifts.

Look for the space between the space. Start to notice that empty space no longer feels empty! It is filled with energy. Be willing to watch your ego scream something like, "You are losing your mind!" and smile at its fearful warnings. When the ego screams, you are most likely on the right track!

WALKING ON WATER

As your own energy vibration becomes more loving and less contaminated with density beliefs, you will find that you naturally begin to lift... to rise above the dramas of the world. It is this lifting energy that will help many thousands anchor in the fifth dimension far ahead of 2012. Those who lead the way serve as Torchbearers for those who come later. That is, their love and their light serve to anchor a frequency of being that others can align with. This is how the new Communities of Light will be birthed into form.

If you are one who is called to quickly move through the strata of consciousness in order to fulfill your heart's call, then this work will offer you momentum. If you are comfortable right where you are, then this work will help you affirm your choice. Trust yourselves and celebrate your knowing. The only opinion that matters is your own!

> You are dimension-shifting, and you are
> gaining access.

Nothing is lost.
In your surrender, all is found.

ARCHANGEL ZADKIEL: ...*step through the wall of Density Consciousness and move into the joyousness of the complete surrender. It is much simpler once one is in complete surrender; the only challenge is walking through that wall. Trust it shall all work out. Trust it shall all be correct.*

Trust that time is very short, very short indeed.

Remember this: every moment is a joyous gift, and that means every moment—this moment, the next moment. Any moment is a joyous gift. This is a time of great celebration for this is the culmination of many millennia, the third expansionary event. It is important for you to understand that it is in every moment that one should be in Joy, every moment!

Anything that does not look like Joy should not be done.

... *and so it is.*

ENDNOTES

This list explains the endnotes that appear throughout the book. Rather than formatted by chapter, they have simply been enumerated sequentially for ease of location.

1   Film, *The Matrix*, 1999 © Warner Brothers, Village Roadshow Pictures.

2   Archangel Zadkiel is credited in the Bible with holding back the hand of Abraham from sacrificing his only son. He is also closely aligned with the energy of the Violet Ray and St. Germain. Attributes held by Archangel Zadkiel are mercy and compassion. We refer to Zadkiel as "He" in this book as the English language does not have a universally understood term for a non-gendered being. In the Kabbalah, Zadkiel's name is said to mean 'Justice of God,' and Joy is his mandate.

3   In-soulment: Uniquely different from channeling, it is direct communion of one soul with another, an ancient process of Angelic communication that completely removes egoic barriers (also review lengthier description at the end of Chapter One).

4   Over 75% of Americans believe in Angels. (*Time* magazine poll, Dec. 1993)

5   The Elohim are the manifested essence of God, without gender or number. In Hebrew, the word Elohim relates to deity and it is the plural of God. It is the third word in the Hebrew text of Genesis, and is found frequently throughout the Hebrew Bible and King James Version of the Bible. Elohim is a plural form but it is used with singular verbs and adjectives in the Hebrew text when the meaning of a singular deity is traditionally understood. Through ages of time, the Elohim have successfully assisted mankind in the creative powers of thought, feeling, spoken word, and action—as God (source) intended them to be used from the beginning.

6   Film, *Indiana Jones and the Last Crusade*; TM & Copyright © 1989 Lucasfilm, Ltd. (LFL).

7   This is the Mantra of Self-Ascension, as gifted to us from the Archangelic Realm.

I am here, I am ready, I am open, Guide me.

8 Archangel Zadkiel has revealed that the commonly-referred-to Atlantis was initially on Mars long before the energies of that experience were brought to this planet. There was also an Atlantis on Earth, quite distinct from the original Atlantean experience.

9 Born on August 12, 1831, Helena Blavatsky (or Madame Blavatsky) was the founder of Theosophy, largely misunderstood, and greatly ahead of her time. She was a great authority on Theosophy, and wrote two monumental spiritual works, *Isis Unveiled* and *The Secret Doctrine*. She was born of Russian nobility and did much to spread Eastern religious philosophical and spiritual concepts throughout the Western world.

10 Sri and Kira's first book

11 We refer to Archangel Zadkiel as "He" in this book as the English language does not have a universally understood term for a non-gendered being. Also, often after hearing Archangel Zadkiel speak, many attribute a masculine energy to the voice being heard.

11 Largely misunderstood by Western culture, the benefits of sun-gazing are numerous and have withstood the tests of time. We were provided with many safe and energizing ways to enjoy sun-gazing from the Archangelic Realm. We have also subsequently sought other confirming evidence of the benefits of sun-gazing. For more information, we suggest that you read *Living on Sunlight, the Art and Science of Sun-Gazing as Taught by Hira Ratan Manek* (also known as HRM).

13 www.selfascension.com

14 Now imagine the possibility that volcanic action will actually lift the ocean bottoms, generating an even higher rise in sea levels before 2012. Our clairvoyant Visions have offered this probability to us. The result is initially devastating, and will awaken many hearts to action.

15 *Sacred Union: The Journey Home:* Chapter Five, The Habit of the Habit of the Pain of the Pain *(page 57).* "It is the ego that helps you believe you must be in pain about the pain."

16 The Archangelic Realm refers to those beings of light who have chosen the experience of density expansion as The Travelers.

17 Referring to the first Atlantean existence; see note 9.

18 Refer to explanation within note 9.

19 See note 20.

20 As light beings expanding, we have had three primary collective experiences of density. Each of these experiences has subsequently created greater density. The first experience was known as Tu'Laya (Leumeria); the second, Atlantis; and the third, this planet, Earth. On this planet there have been expansive experiences that are often referred to as Mu (Leumeria), Atlantis, and the present. These Earth expressions are all based upon earlier energies.

21 The word experiment here refers to the greater expansion as beings of light experiencing density. With each experience of density, light expands ever more as a means of returning love to as wholeness with the Divine.

22 At the fall of the Atlantean experience, energies were transmitted to Earth that would reconnect many with their light experiences at a later time in evolution. These were experienced during the early dynastic and Old Kingdom periods of Ancient Egypt.

23 The Merkabah is an energy vehicle that allows for travel and direct communion with other dimensions and the Beings who reside there. Used with reverence, the Merkabah offers a demonstration of spiritual progress and the ability to witness the vastness of Creation. The Merkabah Revolution describes the time when this sacred vehicle of Divine Communion was instead used as a status symbol by the rich and powerful, who seduced the egos of the keepers of the Divine Wisdom.

Merkabah travel in Atlantis became food for the ego, not a service of the soul. When Atlantis began to decay, some thought they could simply travel away to another world. However, the Elohim eliminated that opportunity as it was recognized that the Atlanteans needed more time to grow as galactic citizens before intermingling with the galactic community. We are at the time now of the reactivation of Merkabah travel energies.

24 The illusion referred to here is the one that assumes this world to be the real world, that we are solid matter, and that we are our physical form.

25 *In Sacred Union: The Journey Home,* Chapter Six, page 76, we discussed the many false gods. One of these false gods is time. "For with the acceptance of time and the belief in this system, one has judgment about the perception of completion. One then believes in aging, one then believes in death, one believes in the concept of control, and one believes in all matters regarding finality...in your modern world, time has become a god. It is the ultimate disconnection."

26 The word Divine is used throughout this book as the expression of God, Eternal, Source, Krishna, Buddha nature, etc. Use whichever term your alignment with the Divine expresses as each time you see this mentioned. Any Divine designation is appropriate.

27 Meister Eckhart was a 14th-century Christian mystic. This quote is taken from page 160 of *Two Suns Rising: A Collection of Sacred Writings.*

28 The third dimension is expressed as the experience we are now living, and includes this planetary existence, your body, senses, emotions, and all tangible expressions of living on this planet.

29 Many believe the Earth's vibrational rate can be measured by the Schumann Resonance. Since 1980, this resonance is claimed to have been slowly rising, and is currently over 12 cycles per second! (The equivalent of having fewer than 16 hours to complete the work of a 24-hour day.) This is also why time seems to be going so fast. The Schumann Resonance itself does not adequately describe celestial time. It is best to simply recognize that we are processing larger quantities of information than ever before and that linear time itself is changing.

30 The concept of Intelligent Design is that humans must have originated from a higher being or source.

31 Our will is an expression of the Divine Will. Through expressing choice we exercise our free will and co-create pain and destruction as well as harmony. Noninterference is respectful, and it supports our learning.

32 Fourth-dimensional beings, often called the Illuminati, believe that the refraction of light into density has contaminated the light. Thus,

they also believe that those who have contaminated themselves should not reunify.

33 The Model of Self-Ascension is foundational work for the path of Self-Ascension, and the basis of our first book, *Sacred Union: The Journey Home*. The four steps around the outside of the Merkabah have no particular order and, once embraced, lead to the inner resolution, shown inside the Merkabah.

Self-Ascension Model
Four Steps for the Journey Home

Be In Union

Release Judgement

Peace Knows God
Love Connects with God
Joy Embraces God

Surrender

Unconditional Love

34 See "Do I have to be a vegetarian to raise my consciousness?" on page 155.

35 Also referred to as the Elohim; see note 5.

36 The central state of Self-Ascension as demonstrated in the Self-Ascension Model.

37 The traditional chakra system subscribes to seven points of energy that align within the body, beginning at the base of the spine. The energies of the lower three are commonly associated with issues of safety (chakra one), sex (chakra two), and power (chakra three).

38 The traditional root chakra is the energy center located at the base of the spine, and is commonly referred to as the first chakra, aligning with the energy of basic needs and/or safety. The root of the Ascended State is the heart, or fourth chakra.

39 Currently known as the throat chakra, which is traditionally the fifth chakra and located at the area of the throat.

40 This is a reference to the first and second chakras of the Ascended State (the fourth and fifth chakras of the traditional system). When Love and Truth are aligned, the doorways to higher consciousness open.

41 Chakras have colors associated with them that assist with the expression of the energies they carry. The Ascended Chakras also have colors, as described.

42 Archangel Zadkiel defines us as having refracted many times from our origin. The example he often uses to describe the process is a crystal in the light. When you hang a crystal in the stream of the sun, it will refract and display many beautiful streams of color.

43 Metatron is an Archangel and a Seraphim, who sits beside God. His primary task is to maintain the eternal archives of the Lord. The Metatron is a reference to the highest Archangel of the Kabbalah at Kether, or the crown.

44 Karma is traditionally recognized as the energetic ramifications of an action. If you create an energetic imbalance through your actions, then you must balance that action in this lifetime. Should the imbalance not be corrected prior to death, than you will be born into another lifetime to complete the necessary balance of energy.

45 See note 15.

46 The Archangelic Realm has taught that we have had three expressions of density: Tu'Laya (Leumeria), Atlantis, and the present time on Earth.

47 The crown chakra is located at the top of the head in the area where Divine Connection is often established, received, and maintained.

48 The solar plexus is the area just below the center of the ribcage.

49 He is referring to the traditional first three chakras, which are "released" in the Ascended State.

50 Ley lines are alignments of ancient sites stretching across the globe via land. Ancient sites or holy places may be situated in a straight line ranging from one or two to several miles in length. A ley may be identified simply by an aligned placing of marker sites,

or it might be a source of energetic experiences that are in alignment with other sites around the world. Often, phenomena of an unexplainable nature seem to congregate at the center points.

51 The word Yoga comes from the Sanskrit word "Yuj" (to yoke, or unite), and is generally translated as Union, or Integration. According to Yoga experts, the Union referred to is that of the individual soul with the cosmos, or the Supreme. Yoga has both a philosophical and a practical dimension. The philosophy of Yoga (Union) deals with the nature of the individual soul and the cosmos, and how the two are related. The practice of Galactic Yoga traditions is specifically designed to bring you closer to this mystical Union.

52 Reprinted with permission from Sacred Union: The Journey Home.

53 Siddhi is a Sanskrit term for spiritual power (or psychic ability). These spiritual powers range from relatively simple forms of clairvoyance to being able to levitate, teleport, be invisible, precipitate objects, have access to memories from past lives, and more.

54 See event-response loop, page 84.

55 Gaia is the Earth as our mother, the energy of she who nourishes all.

56 See Note 32.

57 *Sacred Union: The Journey Home*, page 128.

58 The Yumi Soul is the union of a "You" and a "Me." (*Sacred Union: The Journey Home*, page 144.)

59 *Sacred Union: The Journey Home*, page 117.

60 Polyamory is the philosophy and practice of romantically loving more than one other person at a time. Usually this involves multiple relationships simultaneously, with open understanding between all partners.

61 See note 33 and the accompanying diagram.

62 This teaching is from the Suph'alla, also known as the Benevolent Ones, whose lessons from the Galactic Encyclopedia will be shared more fully in future books. You may also read more from them at our website, www.selfascension.com, *Lessons from the Galactic Encyclopedia*.

63 A way of being based upon the life of Enoch. Enoch was a prophet who lived from 3284-3017 B.C. Enoch's name signifies, in Hebrew, Initiate or Initiator. Due to his devotion to God, he was considered to be the first ascended man, and after spending 300 years with God, returned to teach the men of Earth the reality of the Kingdom of Heaven.

64 Archangel Uriel is the head of the third order or company of Angels. Uriel is often referred to as the Great Archangel of the Earth. Qabalists assign Uriel to the middle pillar of the Tree of Life, and specifically to the sephirah Malkuth, the Kingdom. Malkuth is often associated with the Shekinah, the Glory of God and the Divine Presence in the world. Uriel personifies the Divine Fire that comes down from the Third Aspect of Deity—Universal Mind—penetrating each plane until it reaches the physical.

65 *The Secret Doctrine*, Volume 2, page 446.